The Light-Worker's Companion

Arcadia Press

The Light-Worker's Companion

© Copyright Amanda Guggenheimer 2005, 2011

All rights reserved.

This work is copyright. Apart from any use as permitted under the *Copyright Act 1968,* no part may be reproduced, copied, scanned, stored in a retrieval system, recorded or transmitted, in any form or by any means, without the prior written permission of the publisher.

First Published 2005

Second edition 2011

ISBN 1-921019-29-8

For more information: www.thelightworkerscompanion.com

Published by Arcadia Press

www.arcadiapress.com.au

Country of publication: Australia

Cover design James Terry, Arcadia Press design studio

The Light-Worker's Companion

A Gateway into
Higher Realms and the Dimensions of
Consciousness

Revised Edition

AMANDA GUGGENHEIMER

OTHER BOOKS BY AMANDA GUGGENHEIMER
Tobias and the People of the Sky Realms – Volume I

Do...

- Topics such as philosophy, metaphysics, religion and spirituality call you now more so than ever before?

- You crave reading material and in depth discussion on the above issues?

- You have thought-provoking, insightful, futuristic or even disturbing dreams?

- You experience a strange lethargy at unusual times of the day as though someone has unplugged and then plugged you in again?

- Some friendships seem no longer compatible?

- You have a lack of interest in pushing forward to keep up with the Joneses?

- You have a desire to be in nature?

- People and literature keep appearing that relate to personal and spiritual discovery?

- You crave time alone or with genuine and loving people only?

- You find that communication is becoming increasingly more important to you, yet at the same time recognise challenges in truly connecting with others?

- You find that your body is going through shifts that are hard to explain?

- You talk to a higher power, or guiding spirit more frequently now than before?

If you answer yes to most of these 'symptoms', welcome, you are awakening to your true destiny...

As a Light-Worker you have agreed to awaken earlier than many, to pave the way, to clear debris from the path. This handbook has been designed to aid you in your task.

Contents

The Light-Worker's Companion iii

Introduction
St Germain and the Spiritual Hierarchy for Earth 1

Chapter One
An Introduction to Your Hierarchy 5
   Overview 5
   Learning About Your Hierarchy 10
   Consciously Connecting to Your Hierarchy 11
   Some Key Points About Your Hierarchy 11
   Aligning to Your Hierarchy 12
   Meditation for Connecting to Your Hierarchy 14

Chapter Two
The Earth/Physical Level of The Hierarchy 17
   First Dimension 18
   Second Dimension 18
   Third Dimension 18

Chapter Three
The Etheric Level of The Hierarchy 20
   The Higher Self and Incarnation Team 22
   The Incarnation Council 23
   Council of Balance and Justice 24
   The Higher Council of Higher Self 25

Chapter Four
The Etheric Level Continued The Spiritual Home of Your Mental Plane 26
   The Star Core Command 26
   Lifting the Vibration of Your Mental Field 28

Chapter Five
The Galactic Level of The Hierarchy 31
   Planetary Councils 32
   The Galactic Councils 32
   The Council of Twelve 33

The Council of The Mothership	35
The Council of the Directorship of the Rays	36

Chapter Six
The Upper Galactic Level of The Hierarchy — 37
The Fifth Dimension	37
Christ Consciousness	37
The Sun Level	38
Strengthening Your Connection to the Sun Level and Christ Consciousness	38
The Sixth Dimension	39
The Shambhala Council	39
Connecting with the Shambhala Level	40

Chapter Seven
The Universal Level of The Hierarchy — 41
The Seventh Dimension	41
The Ray Being Level	42
The Universal Level	42
The Soul Level	42
What to Expect as Your Awareness Expands	43

Chapter Eight
Understanding Incarnation — 45
The First Way	45
The Second Way	47
The Third Way	48

Chapter Nine
Assignments of the Human Incarnate — 50
The Torch Bearer	50
The Circuit Breaker	51
The Way-Shower	52
The Light-Worker	53

Chapter Ten
Exploring Ascension — 55
The Ascension Process	55
Earth Assignments	56
First Stage of Ascension	58
The Second Stage of Ascension	60
The Third Stage of Ascension	60

Tools and Techniques to Assist in Ascension ... 63

Chapter Eleven
Ascension and Life Changes ... 65
   Ascension and Social Groups ... 65
   Ascension and Preference ... 66
   Ascension and Time ... 67
   Ascension and Responsibility ... 68
   Ascension and Love ... 69

Chapter Twelve
Aspect Therapy ... 71
   Healing as Ascension ... 71
   Aspect Therapy Meditation ... 73

Chapter Thirteen
Past Life Resolution and Aspect Therapy ... 75
   Past Life Aspect Therapy Meditation ... 79

Chapter Fourteen
The Earth and Sea Realms ... 82
   The Support of The Earth ... 82
   The Triad of the Earth, the Seas and the Nature Realms ... 82
   The Sea Realms ... 83
   The Oceanic Realms and Healing ... 84
   Meditation for Connecting to the Earth and Oceanic Realms ... 85
   Earth ... 88

Chapter Fifteen
The Spiritual Family ... 90
   Meeting the Family ... 90
   The Messenger of Light ... 90
   The Divine Overseer ... 91
   Christ Consciousness Companion ... 92
   Seventh Dimensional Assistance ... 93
   The Brotherhood of Light ... 93
   The Sacred Nuns of the Essene Order ... 93
   The Celestial Archangel Realm ... 95
   The God and Goddess Higher Council ... 96
   Ancient Spiritual Family ... 97
   Ascended Masters ... 98
   Building a Stronger Connection with the Masters and Spiritual Family ... 99

Chapter Sixteen
Guides and Guardians – Their Profiles — 101
- Djwhal Khul — 101
- Sanat Kumara — 103
- St Germain — 104
- Quan Yin — 105
- Lord and Lady Lemuria — 106
- Lord and Lady Gaia — 108
- Lord and Lady Tansafarie — 111
- Lord and Lady Israel — 114
- Mother Mary — 117
- The Celtic Lord of the Forests — 118
- Lord and Lady Avalon — 119
- Lord and Lady Jerusalem — 122
- Lord and Lady Maitreya — 124
- Lord and Lady Neptune — 127
- Lord and Lady Amphibian — 129
- Lord and Lady Sebastian — 130
- Lord and Lady of the Lake — 132
- Lord and Lady Savatar — 134
- How to Connect to the Beings of Light Supporting You — 136

Chapter Seventeen
Spiritual Awareness and Your Physical Life — 139
- Keys to Deepening Your Spiritual Life — 140
- What are the Benefits of Building a Spiritual Life? — 140
- For Spiritual Life, Develop a Tool Box — 142

Chapter Eighteen
Conclusion — 146

Appendix
Suggestions on the Use of Aromatherapy Oils for Spiritual Development — 147

Definition of Terms — 150

Postscript
St Germain — 158

INTRODUCTION

St Germain and the Spiritual Hierarchy for Earth

I, St Germain will now speak to you of the writings you are about to discover. We have created this book to heal and reawaken you, the initiate, to reconnect to your Higher Self and Hierarchy. These teachings are designed to be combined with other spiritual or personal development systems that you may already have in place. Our system shall assist in increasing your awareness of a natural spiritual process that is occurring in you automatically. We call this process Ascension.

Ascension is the process of spiritual awakening. It is where an initiate connects both to the spiritual realms above and the holy realms within. The initiate remembers the higher plan for Earth as well as his/her own divine plan and purpose for being on Earth. Ascension can be an uncomfortable process as it requires the initiate to break away from all that is known or old patterns, belief systems and behaviours that are not compatible with the Ascension process.

We have tried to reduce the level of challenge you experience through education and practical techniques. We explain many factors of the Spiritual Hierarchy for Earth that we have not previously revealed to humanity. We recognise that it is now time for humanity to understand these factors and transcend the fear of the unknown through the gaining of knowledge and awareness. Our reluctance to reveal information in the past has not been a withholding. Rather, it has been a process allowing humanity gradually to integrate new levels of information. We do this progressively as humanity demonstrates it has reached the next stage of personal and broader spiritual awareness where such information is relevant and in alignment with the next phase of development.

Humanity is now ready for the next phase. You, the Light-worker, are now awakening to a new level of awareness. The light that awakens in you as a result of this will light the way for others. Your role as a Light-worker shall become clearer and stronger as humanity moves towards higher levels of awareness or through Ascension. As a Light-worker you have agreed to awaken earlier than others and clear the way for their unfolding. This manual has been designed to prepare you for your task. It is a guide book to assist in your own awakening so that your role as a Light-worker can be truly realised. As a Light-worker you use awareness, light, love and wisdom as your sword. You cut through limitation and become the bridge between the Higher Realms and Humankind.

If you doubt whether you are a Light-worker, know this: if you were not, or were not yet ready for such information, you would not be attracted to this book. Its frequency would not resonate with you. You have been called by your Higher Self to remember your Highest Path. We are honoured to aid you to realise it. We cannot walk your path for you as you cannot walk another's path, nor can we give you all the clues at once. We can however, Light the Way, for you as you will do for others.

The information outlined in this work is relevant for this current time and space. As you attain deeper awareness, you are compelled to engage spiritual principles at new and deeper levels. As you come to deeper levels of awareness, it can feel as though the previous levels you have known are incorrect. This is not the case as those previous levels were relevant at the time, however as you ascend you require new depth and insight. What served you once might now seem obsolete. The process your Higher Self uses to assist you to ascend is ever changing. Allow this natural process of change as you follow your spiritual path. Even with our information, nothing is set in stone; the universe is continually evolving. With this flexibility of mind you will flow easily and joyfully along your path.

I, St Germain send my love to you. I trust that the journey you embark upon as you embrace this book will assist you to reconnect to levels of your Higher Self and inner wisdom. All Beings of Light who have participated in the creation of this work shall be with you when needed as you take each step in this adventure. If at any time you require further assistance in your own development or in understanding the material, call upon us through the process of prayer and meditation. At all times there will be a Being of Light beside you as you work through the material in this book. I, St Germain thank you on behalf of the Spiritual Hierarchy for Earth, for the opportunity to be of service to you through this work. We have faith that you shall feel our love as you move through this process.

A Gateway into Higher Realms

DIAGRAM 1
YOUR HIERARCHY

Soul Level

Home of the
'Ray Being'
Self

Universal Level Begins

Shambhala Level

Sun Level

Council of the
Directorship of
the Rays

Council of the
Mothership

Council of Twelve

Galactic
Councils

Planetary
Council

Star Core
Command

Higher Council
of Higher Self

Council of
Balance and
Justice

Incarnation Council

Etheric Level Begins

Higher Self and
Incarnation Team

Human Incarnation

THE LIGHT-WORKER'S COMPANION

DIAGRAM 2
YOUR HIERARCHY

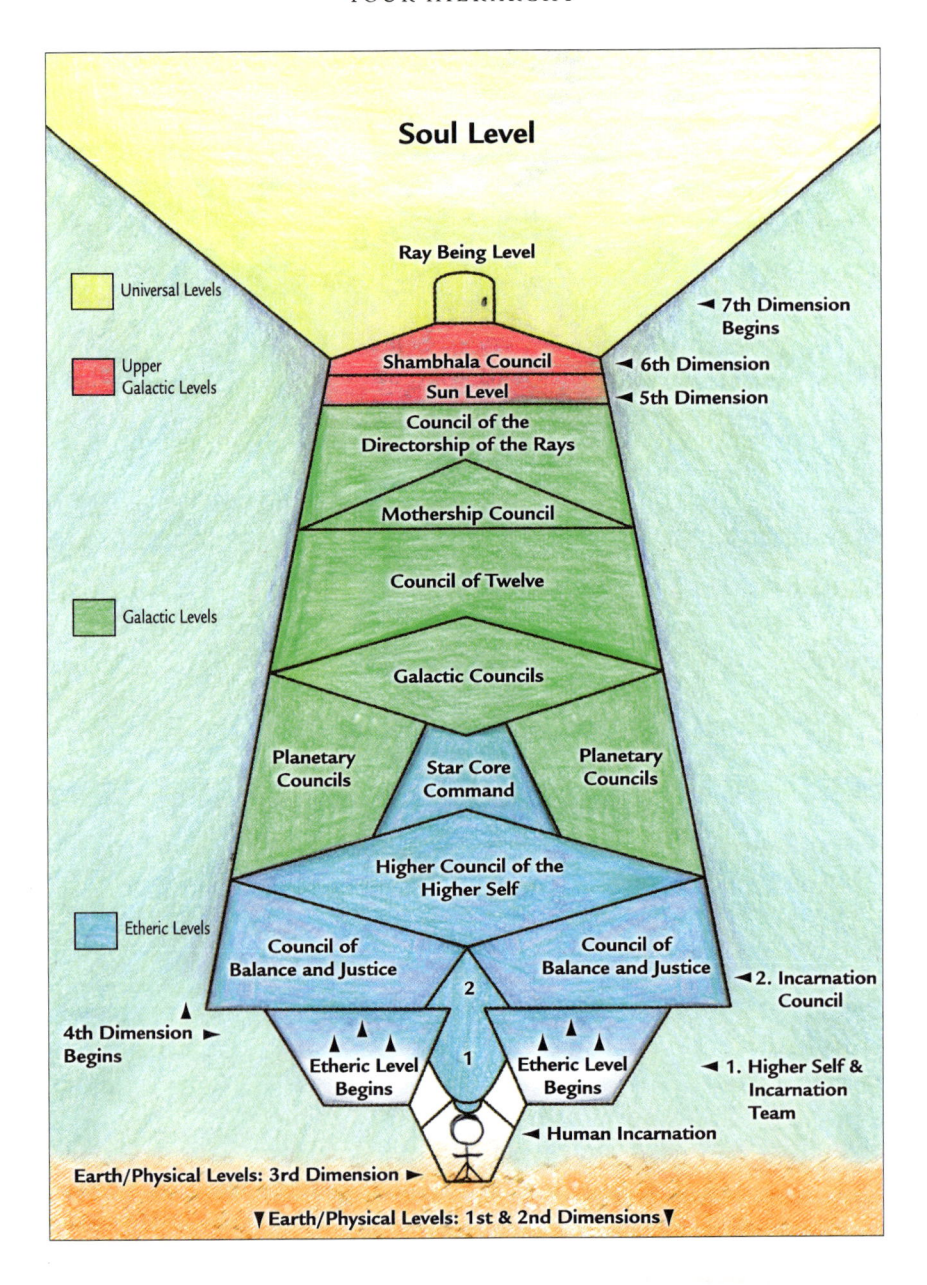

Soul Level

Ray Being Level

◄ 7th Dimension Begins

Universal Levels

Upper Galactic Levels

Shambhala Council ◄ 6th Dimension
Sun Level ◄ 5th Dimension

Council of the Directorship of the Rays

Mothership Council

Council of Twelve

Galactic Levels

Galactic Councils

Planetary Councils — Star Core Command — Planetary Councils

Higher Council of the Higher Self

Etheric Levels

Council of Balance and Justice — Council of Balance and Justice
◄ 2. Incarnation Council

4th Dimension Begins ►

Etheric Level Begins — 1 — Etheric Level Begins
◄ 1. Higher Self & Incarnation Team

2

◄ Human Incarnation

Earth/Physical Levels: 3rd Dimension ►

▼ Earth/Physical Levels: 1st & 2nd Dimensions ▼

A GATEWAY INTO HIGHER REALMS

DIAGRAM 3

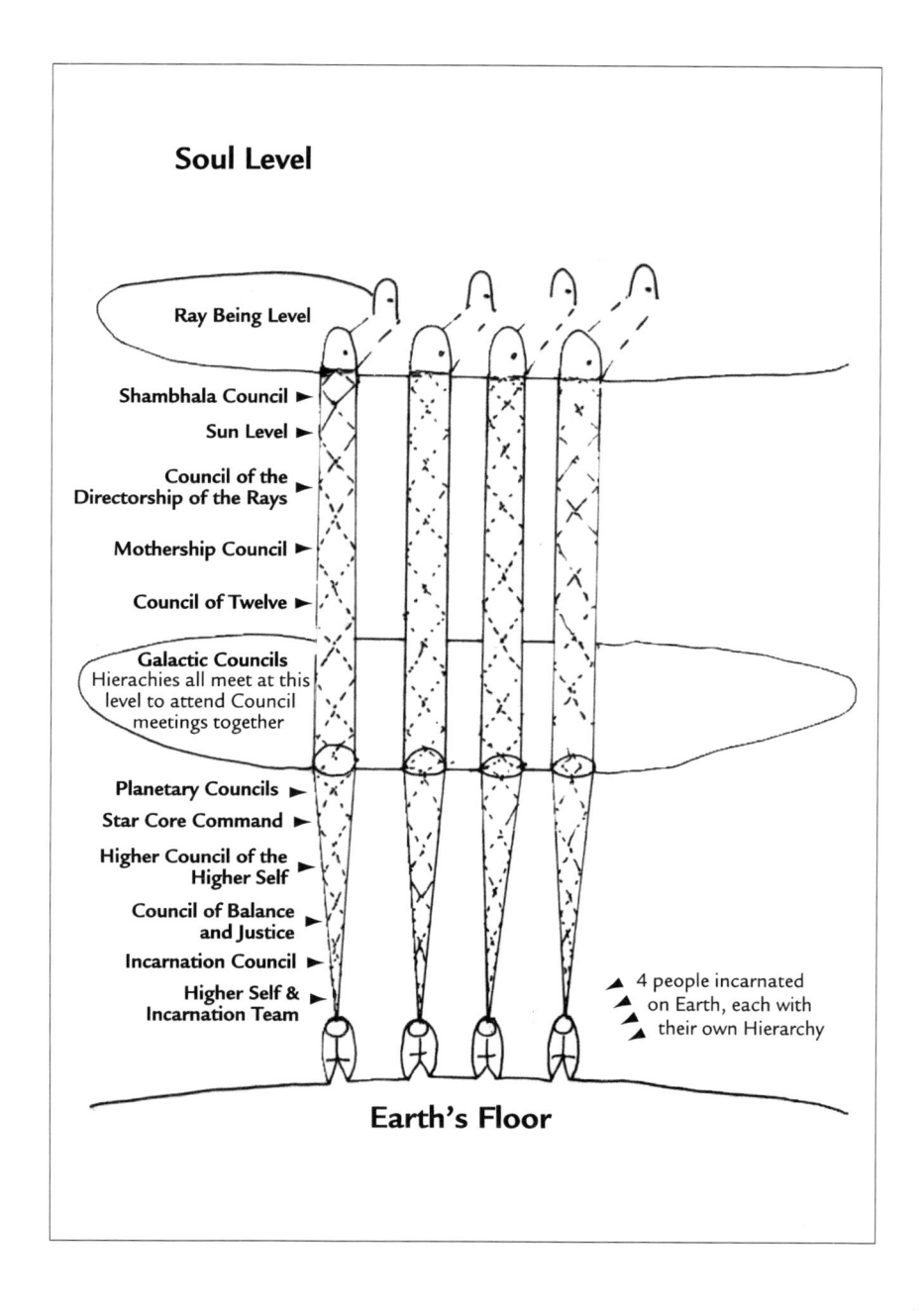

Soul Level

Ray Being Level

Shambhala Council ▶
Sun Level ▶
Council of the
Directorship of the Rays ▶
Mothership Council ▶
Council of Twelve ▶

Galactic Councils
Hierachies all meet at this
level to attend Council
meetings together

Planetary Councils ▶
Star Core Command ▶
Higher Council of the
Higher Self ▶
Council of Balance
and Justice ▶
Incarnation Council ▶
Higher Self &
Incarnation Team ▶

▲ 4 people incarnated
▲ on Earth, each with
▲ their own Hierarchy

Earth's Floor

THE LIGHT-WORKER'S COMPANION

DIAGRAM 4

The Hierarchy

◄ Incarnation Council

◄ Higher Self and Incarnation Team

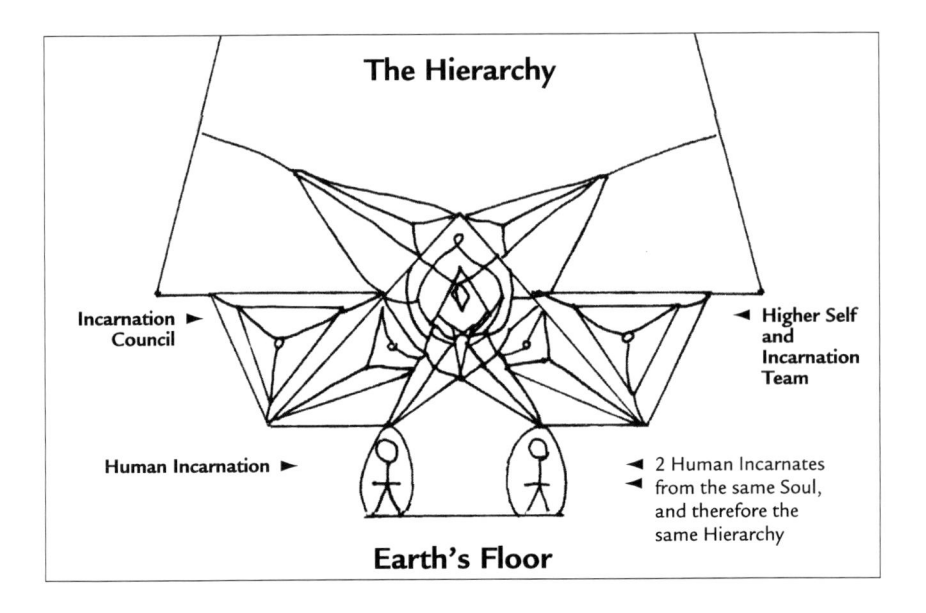

◄ Human Incarnation

◄ 2 Human Incarnates from the same Soul, and therefore the same Hierarchy

Earth's Floor

DIAGRAM 5

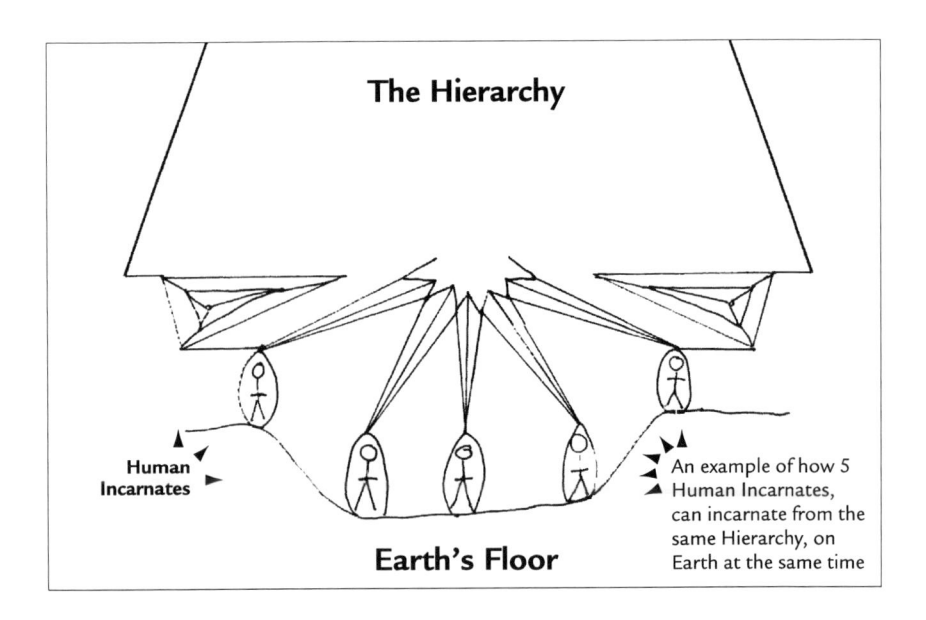

The Hierarchy

◄ Human Incarnates

◄ An example of how 5 Human Incarnates, can incarnate from the same Hierarchy, on Earth at the same time

Earth's Floor

CHAPTER ONE

An Introduction to Your Hierarchy

Overview

THE SPIRITUAL HIERARCHY FOR EARTH:

Many humans walk Earth with a very limited awareness of anything beyond their immediate experience. They are aware when they are hungry, tired, thirsty or in pain. Most people go beyond this and are aware when they are stressed, anxious, angry, happy or sad. Some people extend further to being aware of how others are feeling and they are sensitive to general emotional environments. Then there are others who know that there is more to life than what is seen or felt in the physical world. They dare to explore outside what is known and begin to investigate energetic realities. They may investigate the possibility of spiritual realms, afterlife, guides, angels and healing that cannot be logically explained.

These ones 'stumble upon' their Higher Selves, psychic abilities, intuition and meditation. They begin to use these tools to bring peace into their lives and greater awareness. They have a sense that there is more to them than what they have found. Often they are filled with an overwhelming desire to discover what this is. In choosing to read this book, you signal that you are now consciously connecting with your Hierarchy and awakening to a deeper sense of your Spiritual Self. Through understanding how to consciously connect, you can find the parts of yourself you have been searching for.

Our intention in this chapter is to introduce you to a basic understanding and orientate you, towards your own Hierarchy. Your Hierarchy is a tool that will assist you to attain higher awareness and experience. First we shall introduce you to the multidimensional spiritual system and framework that is your Hierarchy. Secondly we shall orientate you towards the workings of your Hierarchy. We will explain how each level works and how it is useful in your day-to-day spiritual life.

Although this system of light is very complex, it is also very accessible. You will discover the more complex dimensions of it through the explorations you undertake on your own. We have included meditations and exercises for this very purpose. Do not be concerned if you do not understand your Hierarchy straight away. The real understanding comes through experiencing it yourself and the meditations will give you that opportunity.

We choose to work primarily with the Hierarchy diagram (diagram 1) as this depicts your Human Self in relation to its higher spiritual structure. It demonstrates that your Human Self is only one part of a multidimensional and geometrical system. The exercises we have included will assist you to deepen your understanding of this system. Some of the exercises will have a stronger effect on you than others. Use the ones that work for you to create your own individual toolbox. The diagram has been designed to give you a physical image of the spiritual system we are introducing you to.

You may have heard the term 'Hierarchy' or 'Spiritual Hierarchy' used in spiritual texts and conversations in the past. We are here to introduce you to the next level of understanding in relation to these terms. The diagram of the Hierarchy is a symbol of expanded awareness. You can see the little stick figure down the bottom of the structure. Many people on Earth only experience themselves as this figure. Throughout their lives they remain oblivious to anything existing above or outside of this; they are only aware of how they feel, or whether they are tired and hungry. They are aware of their 'humanness' but not necessarily of their 'spiritualness'. Our role as you read this book is to awaken you to the levels that you see on the diagram that are above the 'stick figure'.

> **Author's Notes:** My understanding of the Spiritual Hierarchy for Earth and my own Hierarchy is continually adjusting and evolving as I walk along my spiritual path. One thing I have learnt through my dealings

with the guides and guardians who light my way, is that nothing is set in concrete. The moment I think I have got a handle on something they teach me, they take me to the next level and I realise what I thought I knew, was only such a small part of the bigger picture – and I have a sneaking suspicion that it will always be that way!

My current understanding of the Hierarchy is that we each belong to a particular Hierarchy and each of these particular Hierarchies connected to the Earth assignment, come together to create the Spiritual Hierarchy for Earth. The Spiritual Hierarchy for Earth consists of twelve founding individual Hierarchies that were the first to act as the governing body of the planet. Over time the Spiritual Hierarchy for Earth received the membership of new Hierarchies from different parts of the galaxy. The founding members still remain as the Spiritual Hierarchy for Earth and are the core of the governing body.

Because we are humans in this incarnation, we are automatically part of the Human Hierarchy, just as an angel is part of the Angelic Hierarchy. Our own particular Hierarchy is connected to the Human Hierarchy as well as the Spiritual Hierarchy for Earth. The same applies in the case of an angel who has its own Hierarchy which is connected to the Angelic Hierarchy and then to the Spiritual Hierarchy for Earth.

I may belong to a Hierarchy different from my neighbour, however a Hierarchy can send more than one incarnated aspect to Earth, so I may share my Hierarchy with, for example, one hundred other people on Earth at the moment, as might you. (Please refer to diagram 3 for an example of four different Hierarchies existing on Earth simultaneously.)

Every Hierarchy is equal to another, is a self-sovereign, individual organisation in its own right and is connected to the Divine Source of All that Is. Every member in its own Hierarchy is considered equal to other members, and although the Hierarchy is divided into levels, this is because of each level's different functions and not because of 'better than, less than' reasons.

I am uncertain about how many Hierarchies have been added to the Spiritual Hierarchy for Earth since the times of the founding twelve.

It is quite possible that there are more Hierarchies than we can imagine and we each fit into one of these. I have heard some call these Hierarchies 'soul groups'. There are others that do not believe that we have separate Hierarchies at all, but fit instead into one cosmic Hierarchy which is then divided into 'like frequency' Hierarchies such as the Angelic Hierarchy or the Elemental Hierarchy.

I feel that, like a diamond, the Spiritual Family (a broad term to embrace all beings in our universal Family of Light) is multifaceted. At present I resonate with the possibility that there is a great cosmic Hierarchy that has many levels and exists through all realms and dimensions; it is the manifested form of the All that Is. From this great cosmic Hierarchy there are many Hierarchies, like branches on a tree. The Spiritual Hierarchy for Earth is one branch. From this one branch there are many sub branches and these form the particular Hierarchies within the Spiritual Hierarchy for Earth, like your Hierarchy or mine. From these sub branches or particular Hierarchies other 'Orders' are formed by taking members from each of the Hierarchies and creating, for example, the Angelic Hierarchy.

At the top or Ascension point of each individual Hierarchy, the great Soul from which the Hierarchy extends gathers with the Souls of the other Hierarchies. This is called the Soul Level, and it is here, where the great souls meet, that the Hierarchical form ceases to exist and all become one.

In *'Initiation – Human and Solar'*, Alice Bailey refers to these terms: "That group of spiritual beings on the inner planes of the solar system who are the intelligent forces of nature, and who control the evolutionary processes. They are themselves divided into twelve Hierarchies. Within our planetary scheme, the earth scheme, there is a reflection of this Hierarchy which is called by the occultist, the Occult Hierarchy. This Hierarchy is formed of chohans, adepts, and initiates working through their disciples, and, by this means, in the world." (Lucis Publishing Company, glossary, page 218)

Or earlier in the same work: "The twelve creative Hierarchies are themselves but subsidiary branches of the one cosmic Hierarchy. They form but one chord in the cosmic symphony..." (page 4)

When I have taught workshops on 'Connecting to your Hierarchy', the question is invariably asked "Why do I need to know this? Or, How does knowing about my Hierarchy help me solve the problems in my life?" Understanding your Hierarchy is not necessary in orchestrating the practical aspect of everyday life, but it can enrich your life. It can give you a basic understanding of some of the spiritual systems that organise human life.

Through communicating with my Hierarchy I have been assisted to make choices about events and to understand the meaning behind certain occurrences. In meditation I talk to my Hierarchy about issues in my life, decisions to make and other spiritual questions that may arise. I receive the answers I require and emerge from meditation with clarity and a fresh perspective. This deepens my experience of life, as I have the option of approaching earthly issues from a spiritual perspective, thus removing the fear, drama or confusion out of the matter at hand.

People have always known that there are higher sources of wisdom, whether or not they call them 'Spiritual Hierarchies', but have not always had access to empowering frameworks in which to understand their workings or the fundamental universal principles that govern the Higher Realms and life on Earth alike. Thus there has been through time great fear around spirituality, with the few people who claim to be the bridge between the people and the divine holding all the power. Man's rules and beliefs have been projected onto the divine, and the people have believed that the Higher Realms must think the same fearful, judgemental and condemning thoughts as humans do.

Instead of relying on some of the fearful belief systems of religious disciplines to know what to do, think and act, or what will happen to me if I don't, I have embraced the Higher Realm's teachings on the Hierarchy as a way of tapping into wisdom from a higher source for myself. Every person is capable of creating such a relationship themselves and we currently live in an age where more and more people are committed to seeking greater connection with the divine.

This doesn't mean that I must reject my traditional religious upbringing – or that you have to abandon yours, but it does provide me with a vast framework in which to pose questions and receive answers in the search for meaning, and there is no reason why it cannot do the same for you, in fact it could even strengthen your connection.

Some of the benefits in understanding the Hierarchy are less tangible than receiving answers to my day-to-day questions, as they answer questions I have carried with me over lifetimes as to the geometry and nature of reality. Understanding the Hierarchy has been the foundation for my understanding of 'what's out there' and what's within me. This has dispelled many of my fears of the 'unknown' about the metaphysical structures governing Earth, such as what happens when I die, spirits and beings, how did I come to be here, and what is the purpose of my past incarnations and current life.

There are also many aspects of learning about my Hierarchy and the Spiritual Hierarchy for Earth that I embrace for the pure enjoyment of it, such as learning about many different realms, kingdoms and the Beings of Light that oversee them. Although I have barely touched the tip of the iceberg in terms of understanding the cosmos, I have received a glimpse of the possibilities within realms through learning about the Hierarchy.

> "There are more things in heaven and earth, Horatio, than are dreamt of in your philosophy." WILLIAM SHAKESPEARE.

Learning About Your Hierarchy

THE SPIRITUAL HIERARCHY FOR EARTH:

Because your Hierarchy exists across all dimensions and levels, it allows for your Soul to experience itself within all dimensions, planetary worlds and realms. Your Soul is your eternal, Original Self from which your Hierarchy extends. Contained within your Soul is your signature frequency, your indestructible essence, your quintessence that cannot be tainted or altered or removed from the Oneness.

Your Soul sends particles of itself down into the Hierarchy structure. These particles choose to incarnate into various forms such as human bodies, animals or energetic beings sometimes, all at the same time. Your Soul can be seen as a sun that sends rays of sunlight down towards Earth and other planetary worlds. The sun ray is the spirit that fills a physical form such as a human body.

These shards of light from your Soul may also volunteer themselves to be light energies that make up the consciousness and may become energetic beings such as Angelic Beings, and Nature Spirits. Some Souls prefer to manifest parts of themselves to become different planetary worlds such as Earth, Venus, and Neptune. They may be the essence of that which is the ocean, or the Earth, the willow tree or the gases of Neptune. We all have so many wonderful choices of how we can experience ourselves in every way over an endless period of time and in a variety of different yet simultaneous expressions.

Souls benefit from manifesting a shard of their light as a human on Earth. It is an opportunity to develop less evolved aspects of the Soul's Hierarchy and contribute to the evolution of humanity. This process has the ability to evolve the whole Soul in a way that brings experience and knowledge. Many people choose to incarnate themselves over and over again in an effort to fulfil the very difficult and challenging goal of awakening to the sacred divine light within, amongst all of the divine earthly diversions. The important thing to remember is that all earthly experiences are transmutable and can always be evolved in a way that brings spiritual evolution to the Soul.

Consciously Connecting to Your Hierarchy

These two exercises assist you to consciously connect to your Hierarchy. The first exercise trains you to become familiar with consciously receiving energy from your Higher Self and feeling connected. As with all meditations in this book, you may wish to read them onto a tape. You can then play the recording back to yourself while in a meditative state.

Some Key Points About Your Hierarchy

- Throughout all of your incarnations, you have always belonged to the same Hierarchy as it is an extension of and part of your Soul.

- You can never be separate from your Soul, or change Souls.

- Your Hierarchy is constructed of geometrical light designs.
- It is made up of colour, sound and light.
- It is balanced within its Masculine and Feminine energies.
- Even though you are on Earth, you are contained within your Hierarchy.
- Every person on Earth is an aspect of a Hierarchy.
- Your Hierarchy is connected to the Spiritual Hierarchy of Earth.

In the case of 'Soul Mates' or being 'one and the same' with your life partner, it is possible that a Soul can send two particles of itself down through the Hierarchy and into incarnation as humans on Earth at the same time. These two people can meet and choose to spend their lives together as incarnations of the same Soul. Because they are from the same Soul, they are from the same Hierarchy.

Sometimes a Soul sends many particles of itself down to be incarnated as humans at the same time but with a different outcome from the 'soul mate' scenario described above. These people may or may not know each other in their lifetimes and may live closely or in different parts of the world, but together, consciously or unconsciously, they are working together to evolve their Hierarchy and Soul as well as to contribute to the healing and spiritual evolution of Earth and Humanity. (Please refer to diagrams 4 and 5)

Aligning to Your Hierarchy

- Close your eyes and breathe deeply.
- Feel calmness wash over you as your breathing relaxes your body.
- Focus on the top of your head. You may feel pressure here or sense that it is starting to glow a white or golden colour.
- Lift your attention beyond your head to high above you in the ethers.
- Sense or see that there is a brilliant source of light out here, beaming love and light to you on Earth.
- Connect with this light and ask it to move closer to Earth towards you.

- As it moves towards Earth, the strength of its light intensifies. You can feel it.
- It is now directly above you.
- As you give this source of light permission, it will move through your body.
- Your body is now filled with the most brilliant gold, white light and highest love.
- This light grounds into your feet and then further down into the core of the Earth.
- As the light moves back up from the core, you feel anchored to the Earth.
- You now have a stream of light travelling down from the ethers into you. There is also light coming up from the Earth, energising you.
- These two energies meet in your heart centre.
- Sit with this feeling for a while, breathe in and then slowly open your eyes.

The second exercise is to use the diagram as a blueprint for your meditations. In a meditative state start at your human self (the stick figure) depicted in the diagram and systematically explore each of the levels. Imagine that you are standing on the ground floor of a multistory building and there is an elevator to take you up into other levels or down into the Earth. On every floor there is a council meeting where you can discuss issues with other aspects of yourself (your Hierarchy). There may be many different projects underway on each floor and many plans being created that will soon manifest in your life on Earth. There are many rooms of filed memory banks where your Hierarchy stores the memories of all of its lifetimes and experiences. The following meditation can be your guide. You may return to this meditation as often as you like to explore different levels of your Hierarchy or to seek guidance from the different councils in relation to life questions that arise for you.

Meditation for Connecting to Your Hierarchy

- Gently close your eyes and move around a little until your body is in a comfortable position.

- Listen to the sounds outside your room.

- These sounds will now fade away and your mind will slowly drift through the different thoughts of the day.

- Your mind will now visit a most magnificent blue shimmering lake surrounded by ancient green mountains.

- You find yourself standing on the soft sandy bank of the lake looking across the water to the mountains.

- The fresh cool air calms your body as you breathe deeply.

- You walk away from the lake and up an old stone trail etched into the Earth.

- Follow the rocky wall of the mountain around until you come to a cave like entrance.

- Move slowly into the depth of the cave leaving the outside world behind you.

- The cave becomes very dark yet comforting as you move deeper and deeper into it.

- Up ahead you see the faint glow of a warm lantern light.

- As you move closer you realise that two lanterns light an entrance of a heavy door. The door looks ancient and in some ways familiar with certain patterns and symbols etched into it.

- The door opens inwards slowly to reveal a marble floor, again with symbols on it.

- As you step onto the marble floor, the large door closes behind you.

- s the floor, you see that you are on what appears to be the or of a multistory building. You look towards the ceiling and realise it is a glass dome structure allowing the sunlight to enter into every aspect of the building.

- There are levels leading up to the dome, and a glass elevator to take you to each level. Beings of light are walking around with scrolls and plans, some in groups, some alone.

- You look towards the centre of the ground floor and see a large round table – a council table. You can sense that there are some Beings of Light spread around the table chatting informally.

- You walk towards the table and sit down gently.

- A Being of Light across the table smiles at you. You know that this being has a special connection with you and in some way feels very familiar.

- The Being of Light stands up from the chair and moves to a seat closer to you. As it does you begin to sense what the Being of Light may look like.

- As it sits next to you, spend some time feeling into the love and the light that it is beaming at you.

- The Being of Light reaches out and takes your hand. As it does this you feel warmth and a gush of love. The being welcomes you home to your Hierarchy.

- Take some time now with the Being of Light to feel into your Hierarchy and have a look around if you wish. The being may show you into certain areas of the Hierarchy and explain the certain areas to you as you go.

- When you are ready, the Being of Light, your spiritual friend, leads you back to the entrance door in which you came in through. You embrace and thank your friend of light and know that you can return whenever you wish to.

- As you step through the door, it closes behind you and you are back in the cave.

- You make your way back through the cave and into the sunlight.

- The sunlight warms and welcomes you as you walk back to the shimmering lake.

- When you are ready to return from the lake, bring your awareness back to your body and to the room or area you are lying in.
- Breathe in deeply to ground your spirit back to earth and gently open your eyes.

Return to explore the many levels of your Hierarchy as often as you feel the need. Allow yourself to develop strong connections with the Beings of Light that come to greet you as you visit your Hierarchy.

CHAPTER TWO

The Earth/Physical Level of The Hierarchy

THE SPIRITUAL HIERARCHY FOR EARTH:

(For this next section we are referring to diagram 1, however, use diagram 2 for further clarification. In diagram 2, the gap between the Earth/Physical Level and the Etheric Levels has not been 'coloured in' to indicate what level the human being is in, because this varies from person to person. For some people it may be relevant to colour the section orange showing the individual is primarily grounded in the third dimension, and for others who have evolved beyond much of the third dimension, they are more connected to the etheric and the gap would need to be coloured in blue to depict this.)

There are many levels to the structure of your Hierarchy, more levels, in fact, than the ones written on the structure diagram. The ones that have been recorded are major levels that have a big impact on the spiritual understanding and development of you, the Incarnated Self. **The Earth/physical** level of the Hierarchy is found within the **first, second and third dimensions**. The **etheric levels** of the Hierarchy **begin at the upper reaches of the fourth dimension, the Human Kingdom**. Humans have the ability to tap into and integrate the etheric levels of their Hierarchy so that they experience an upper fourth and eventually fifth dimensional state whilst living in the third dimensional earthly, physical reality.

First Dimension

The first dimension is home to the mineral kingdom. Creation begins at the embryonic stage and gradually develops into form. All creation in this dimension has consciousness and is connected to and part of the Divine Source. It is very much connected to the Divine Mother having just been born from the Divine Womb.

Having been born from the Divine Womb of the feminine realms of the void, creation in the first kingdom enters into the light of the formed reality being the masculine realms. Thus all creation in the first dimension begins life in the balance of feminine and masculine energies. Being born **from** the womb of the Mother it knows the darkness, the feminine, and **into** the world of the Father it knows the light, the manifestation of the masculine. In the womb where there is the nothingness, creation **knows** itself. In the masculine realms that are light where there is geometric structure, colour, sound and manifested frequencies, creation **experiences** itself.

Second Dimension

The second dimension is home to the plant/vegetable kingdom. In the second dimension creation enters the next level of development. It begins to take its first steps on the path of experiencing itself by entering into the cycles of living: birth, death and rebirth. It realises its presence has an effect on the world as it makes itself recognised and experienced by other forms of creation. It belongs to a community of other forms of creation and can experience itself in relation to this.

Third Dimension

The third dimension can easily be understood as the animal kingdom. The third dimension develops consciousness further into a level of self consciousness. Creation develops an attachment to its life and thus develops the Will to Survive. Such attachment creates awareness of that which may damage or end life and thus fear is born.

The creation teaches itself to experience the duality of safety and fear in an effort to survive and will learn to instinctively sense and feel. To do this it allocates a section of its consciousness to form a survival based intelligence.

This section of the mind's primary role is to develop a system where information may be filed in order to be recalled in an effort to keep the creation in safety. The information filed is its own past experience or the witnessed experience of other creations. A creature will create this information bank in the early stages of its life, drawing on its own experience, and the lessons from its elders or community. This type of intelligence is developed for the purpose of serving the objectives of the Will to Survive.

Humans exist in the third dimension or lower levels of the fourth dimension until they evolve themselves beyond their primary focus on survival and desire to survive, to the more spiritual aspirations of the upper fourth dimension.

The purpose of the Earth/physical level of the Hierarchy is to house the first, second and third dimensions thus creating a foundation for the Hierarchy to evolve aspects of itself, for example, a human initiate, into higher states of consciousness. Once a Hierarchy stabilises itself within these dimensions it will then prepare to incarnate a human being onto Earth to begin the next level of its evolution.

In a very practical way, these dimensions have an important purpose in spiritual development which is often neglected by the human initiate. Regularly in spiritual training, initiates focus intently on connecting 'up' into the Higher Realms and forget that without their Hierarchy first stabilising its position in the first, second and third dimensions, the initiate would not have a foundation from which to evolve. This is where the 'grounding' principle stems from; as an initiate focuses 'up' he must also focus 'down', creating a relationship with the heavenly, celestial realms and the spiritual realms of the Earth equally. As this balance is achieved the initiate develops a new level of connection and awareness of Mother Earth, the natural world and the sea realms, experiencing himself as a very grounded and well rounded individual.

CHAPTER THREE

The Etheric Level of The Hierarchy

Author's Notes: Because of its ethereal nature, the etheric realm is not 'compatible' with the first, second and third dimensions that house dense or solid forms and therefore can only connect to a human once he/she has reached beyond the density of the third dimension and into the fourth dimension. Even then there are many varying levels of awareness in the etheric realm ranging from a vague feeling that there is something else 'out there' to experiencing direct communication from higher spiritual beings. The level of awareness experienced in the fourth dimension, depends on whether the incarnate is content with the lower levels of this dimension, or chooses to move into its higher levels.

When a person chooses to move into the higher levels of the fourth dimension he/she enters into a whole new phase of learning and experience where the belief systems and behaviours that governed the old life of the third and lower fourth dimensions are stripped away. This makes room for the higher frequencies responsible for clear relationship with the Higher Realms.

When I have been asked to define the etheric realm, I have drawn from my own experience of the etheric, being 'that which is not physical but still exists', and realised that it did not suffice as a clear explanation. I then headed for my dictionary, hoping that it could explain something that is often better grasped through the direct experience of it, and for me that has been through meditation.

Ether – 'A hypothetical medium formerly believed to fill all space and to support the propagation of electromagnetic waves. Greek myth: The upper regions of the atmosphere; clear sky or heaven.'

Etheric – (adjective).

Ethereal – 'Extremely delicate or refined; exquisite. Almost as light as air; impalpable; airy. Celestial or spiritual.'[1]

There are many students of metaphysics and the New Age movement who believe humanity is now at a new doorway of consciousness, that critical mass has been achieved and the tipping of the balance will sweep man into the fourth dimension. Others are more sceptical, believing that it will take radical changes before humanity will dare leave the perceived security of the third dimension to look beyond its reaches into the unknown realm of the fourth dimension. What is certain is that whether it takes years, decades or centuries, changes will occur in the mindset of humanity creating connection with higher states of consciousness. The etheric realm is something that we will eventually come to know intimately as a natural function of evolution.

The Spiritual Hierarchy for Earth:

The fourth dimension is known as the Human Kingdom, as the abilities and sensibilities a person aligns to in the fourth dimension reflect the truer nature of humanity than that of the behaviours and beliefs a person adopts as a product of existing in the third dimension.

The fourth dimension is home to the development of consciousness beyond the Will to Survive into more subtle aspects of living and being. It is in this dimension that creation awakens to levels of awareness that pose questions such as "Who am I?", "Where do I come from spiritually?", "Who, What, Where is my Creator?" and "What is my purpose?"

In the fourth dimension, creation seeks to reconnect to and reclaim its Higher Self and its relationship with the divine. The Human Incarnate begins a program initiated by Higher Beings of Light that is designed to

1. *Collins English Dictionary,* (Harper Collins Publishers, Glasgow Great Brittan, 2003)

assist him to awaken to his Higher Self. The Human Incarnate may not initially be aware of the Higher Beings of Light assisting him.

When the incarnate passes these initial awakening training procedures he is then introduced into a series of initiations to shed the foundation of fear established in the third dimension. In the higher levels of the fourth dimension, he is trained to hold the frequencies of the fifth dimension in order to gain entry into the realm of complete Christ Consciousness. He is trained to continually refine his thoughts and actions in preparation for fifth dimensional living. To aid him with his journey through the fourth dimension, the initiate is connected to his own Higher Self and Incarnation Team. This installs in him a sense of the strong network of support being made available.

The Higher Self and Incarnation Team

This level is accessed through the fourth dimension, the beginning of the etheric level of the Hierarchy. It is the gateway into all other spiritual levels and realities and opens up for the initiate, the heightened awareness and spiritual gifts of the fourth dimension. Once you are connected to your Higher Self, you automatically connect to all levels that the Higher Self is connected to. You can see through the diagram of 'your Hierarchy' that the Higher Self is connected to every other part of the Hierarchy due to the geometry of the structure.

As well as being the first point of connection for you, the Incarnated Self, the Higher Self and Incarnation Team takes care to meet your physical needs according to what you have chosen for your earthly experience. This level reads how you are and then relays that information back to the Higher Council of Higher Self. The Higher Self monitors how you are coping with the Earth assignment, how the physical body is responding to different stresses and experiences and whether it needs extra or specific assistance. The Higher Self and Incarnation Team works out which channels, the communication lines between you and your Higher Self, (see 'Channel systems' in the Definitions of Terms section) are integrating, which ones are not, and it also looks after the technical side of the spiritual channelling system of the human body. The Higher Self and Incarnation Team listens to your requests, questions, suggestions, and complaints, and endeavours to find solutions where appropriate.

Your Higher Self is who you are, really, without the learnt behaviours, patterns and beliefs of your earthly personality, or third dimensional self. Your Higher Self is the station into which other aspects of your Hierarchy connect and then reach your physical body. Your Higher Self is the director of the plan for your physicality and your time upon Earth.

The Incarnation Council

Working closely with the Higher Self, the Incarnation Council is concerned with manifesting the essence of your Soul into your human form, and into a blueprint and life plan upon Earth's floor. The Incarnation Council is represented as the orange diamond shaped structure connected to the blue/purple 'head piece' structure which is the Higher Self and Incarnation Team.

The Incarnation Council works closely with the Higher Council of Higher Self, and the Higher Self and Incarnation Team to determine how the blueprint must look in order for your Soul to fulfil all of its tasks. In any one blueprint there are millions of agreements, karmic clearings, and lessons for growth and soul evolution so as you can imagine, this council has a big job! The council addresses important factors in the blueprint such as the parents and sibling agreements, the sex and health of the incarnated self, the environmental, psychological and socio-economic situation of the family and community, and the time and date of birth.

The Higher Self and Incarnation Team will then oversee developments and ensure that all things go according to what was agreed from the birthing procedure to the fulfilment of the life plan.

The Incarnation Council plans 'chance' meetings and more long standing interactions between its Human Incarnate and other people for the purposes of clearing any unresolved issues carried over from previous incarnations, or exchanging keys (vital pieces of information that help you remember your true nature and why you are on the planet – your divine purpose. See the definitions section). The Incarnation Team orchestrates these meetings that the Incarnation Council has planned.

You, the Incarnated Self, can connect with the Incarnation Council in meditation and dreams. During these states you can request advice and information regarding life choices and agreements. You may be faced with a big decision or be at a crossroad where the most beneficial path to take cannot be seen clearly. The council can clarify these powerful times in your life if you are willing to seek advice. Through practice you can learn how to connect to the Council, how to receive clear guidance and then utilise the guidance in life. As you grow in this practice it 'fast tracks' your movement along the life path and you occasionally achieve more than you bargained for with your time on Earth, much to the delight of your Higher Self and Hierarchy.

To connect with your Incarnation Council to receive answers to your life questions, follow the meditation 'Connecting to your Hierarchy' outlined previously. Take the elevator explained in the meditation to the first level of your Hierarchy. Step out of the elevator and into a large room. You will see a council table set up with many seats. Generally there will be Beings of Light at this council. Present your questions or challenges to them and ask for their response. You may hear the answers directly whilst you are in meditation. If you do not, don't be concerned. The answer will always come providing it is in your best interest to know, and will come in dreams or in some other way. The Council will always find a way to communicate with you.

> **Author's Notes:** As already mentioned, you can use this same method of 'taking the elevator', to any council that you choose. Simply step into the elevator and state your intention for the council you wish to visit. The elevator will take you to the level that you need to go to.

Council of Balance and Justice

On either side of the Incarnation Council, underneath the Higher Council of Higher Self is the Council of Balance and Justice. This council acts as a foundation and grounding force for the Higher Councils. It stabilises the consciousness of the Hierarchy through a grounding frequency, making the higher and finer frequencies of the Hierarchy more accessible to the human self. Contained in the Council of Balance and Justice is one of the many councils in the Hierarchy, the Law of One Council. This particular council ensures that all decisions made by the Hierarchy are in harmony with the Council's intention, which is:

> *"When all are allowed to be within their frequencies, all shall come into peace and harmony."*

This intention balances your Hierarchy with other Hierarchies so that every 'individual' decision brings growth and expansion for all. The Council understands that there really are no 'individual' decisions as every choice affects others. The Law of One ensures that Hierarchies make choices that do not encroach on others' aligned will or restrict other Hierarchies the freedom to choose their own expression or 'be within their own frequencies.' The Council understands that this ultimately brings peace and harmony to all.

The Higher Council of Higher Self

The next level of the Hierarchy, The Higher Council of Higher Self is represented as the pink, gold and purple diamond and triangular structure. The Council of Twelve that sits on levels above, works very closely with this council as the twelve members of the Council of Twelve (see Chapter 5) hold offices in the Higher Council of Higher Self. These two councils are responsible for the majority of the decisions made in the Hierarchy. The Higher Council of Higher Self is considered the governing body of the Hierarchy at present, as the focus of the Hierarchy is currently on the Earth assignment and the responsibilities that arise from being part of the Spiritual Hierarchy for Earth.

This council has a practical approach and relies on many beings in the Hierarchy to gather information to aid it with its decision making processes. The Higher Council depends on the Council of Twelve for a second opinion as it is higher in vibration and acts as an overseeing board. There are more members on this council as it has a more hands-on approach in regard to the practical orchestration of its choices, and therefore deals with other practical compartments of the Hierarchy, more so than the Council of Twelve.

The Higher Council of Higher Self is primarily interested in the role of the Hierarchy upon Earth. It keeps in close communication with the Higher Self as a way of monitoring the outcomes of experiences, and progress of its incarnated aspect or aspects.

CHAPTER FOUR

The Etheric Level Continued
The Spiritual Home of Your Mental Plane

THE SPIRITUAL HIERARCHY FOR EARTH:

The consciousness or awareness that you carry with you in your life on Earth has its origins not within your mind but in a higher level of your Hierarchy. In this chapter we will explore your Earth based mental plane, its spiritual home and the effect your thought processes have on your spiritual development.

The Star Core Command

The Star Core Command is the rose coloured heart shape structure nestled in amongst the two green planetary structures, and is responsible for programming the consciousness of your Hierarchy. It sits in the etheric and fourth dimensional levels of the Hierarchy. This command centre channels information and thought forms into the Hierarchy's consciousness to ensure it maintains a unified and harmonious mental vibration. It scans regularly for imbalances in different areas of the Hierarchy's mental body. To do this, it searches for irregular patterns in the mental field. The mental field is like a layer of energy within the Hierarchy and surrounds all of the beings within the Hierarchy including the human self. Some people have evolved the Earth-bound part of their mental field to a 'prayer field' where the field is continually filled with prayers and the highest focused intentions. (See the book 'The Secret of Shambhala' by James Redfield for a deeper understanding of 'prayer fields').

Once the Star Core Command finds irregularities, it transmutes them by first understanding the cause, explores how best to treat it and then implements its plan. The plan may be to change the programming of the mental field, or if the problem is coming from outside the field, strengthen and protect it against negative exterior influences.

To understand the mental field, think of it as an energy field around a living thing. This energy field is partly for the purpose of holding thought forms and regulating awareness and intelligence. The Star Core Command uses your mental field to program you to think differently, question beyond what you are told on Earth and eventually awaken to your spiritual heritage. The mental field contains the thought forms of a Human Incarnate. If this field is weak it may be vulnerable to thought forms and projections within the global consciousness. Humans with weak mental fields may feel harassed by the negative thought forms of others or may feel they struggle to stay above negative attitudes within the psyche of humanity.

The Star Core Command channels higher information down into the Lunar Mind of the Human Incarnate. The Lunar Mind is the feminine aspect of the mind responsible for receiving divinely inspired information. (Also see the Definitions section.) The Star Core Command enlightens the human self slowly over time by charging it with upgraded information and thought forms received through the Lunar Mind.

The Higher Council of Higher Self and the Council of Twelve are both responsible for decisions regarding changes to the programming of the consciousness of the Hierarchy. Changes to any part of the mental body/fields of the Hierarchy and its aspects are given a lot of consideration in council meetings as thought forms are very powerful things. To better grasp how the Star Core Command works, see it as a series of rooms filled by a computer system where beings in the Hierarchy continually send telepathic communication through channels to other parts of the Hierarchy, and through the Lunar Mind, to the Human Incarnate.

Although the Star Core Command is responsible for programming the consciousness of the Hierarchy, this does not mean that the Human Incarnate is not responsible for his/her thought forms. Ascension is aided considerably by transforming negative or lower thought forms and replacing them with positive, higher and harmonious thoughts. Many believe that this process is the most important in Ascension and one cannot ascend until one's thought forms reflect higher states of consciousness.

While the Star Core Command is always available for assistance in the usual way (through meditation), you can contribute significantly to raising the vibration of your own mental field in a very direct way yourself. The following exercises will help cleanse you of the negative thought forms floating around in the mass consciousness. They also lift any negative thoughts that you yourself may harbour. The three accessible tools you can use to raise the vibration of your mental field are sound, thought and cleansing aids.

Lifting the Vibration of Your Mental Field

Sound

In your meditations use the vibration of sacred chants to create a force field of sound vibration in and around you. The AUM chant is very powerful and has been used by initiates for centuries. Start by breathing in. Very slowly make the sound of A and gradually merge it with the sound of U. Hold that sound and then bring in the M sound. When you have finished keep your eyes closed and feel the vibration of the sound all around you. Start again, repeating the chant. You can do this for as long as you like.

Purchase a Tibetan Monk Chanting compact disc or tape. Play it as you meditate. To raise the mental energy in your home, have it playing throughout your house for a day. If there have been arguments in your home or you have been feeling a little down at home, play the sounds on repeat throughout the house until you start to feel the energy lift.

You may find that other types of music have a similar effect. Always choose what works for you. For example, the beat of tribal drums, the high notes of an opera singer, or the sacred Aboriginal sounds of the didgeridoo. Use these sounds often as they are exceptional tools for raising mental vibration.

Thought

Raise your mental field by introducing higher thought forms on a regular basis. Positive affirmations are accessible and can be fun. Stick quotes and images around your home where you will see them often. Have 'angel cards' or positive affirmation cards in a bowl in your home or work place where you can pick them up and look at them often.

Read spiritual and personal development books as a way of reprogramming your thinking processes.

Gradually change your self talk over from 'I can't', 'I hate', 'I'm no good at' to 'I can', 'I love', 'I embrace'. Do this with the use of positive affirmations and use them regularly. 'I love who I am' and 'I am a loving and happy person' are wonderful thoughts to have and repeat to yourself as you move about your day to day tasks.

Deeper seeds of self-doubt in your mind maybe due to unresolved aspects of yourself. This is addressed in chapter 12.

Cleansing Aids for Yourself and Home

- Crystal, flower, fruit and herb essences and aromatherapy oils can lift negative thought forms quickly.

- Burn aromatherapy oils in an oil burner at home or work to transmute lower thought forms and energies. If the issue is thought and emotion-related, combine Orange, Lavender and Rosemary oils together.

- Place amethyst and clear quartz crystals in areas of the house that you intuitively feel need cleansing. These crystals will also replenish the energy of tired house plants – plants work to transmute negativity in your home. Place the crystals in the tops of the plant pots. If there have been arguments around the dinner table, place the crystals in the centre of the table or in a pot plant at the edge of the table.

- Bunches of Rosemary around the home and under the bed will dispel negative thought forms.

- Combine drops of aromatherapy oils in a spray bottle with water and spray your energy field and home regularly. This will keep the energy in your home and energy field clear.

- Soak in a bath with Epsom salts, sea/rock salts, Lavender, Rosemary and Orange (use fresh herbs and fruit, or if using aromatherapy oils, dilute in a dash of milk) to lift debris and restore your mental field. If you have sensitive skin, limit the oils to only a few drops in the bath, or choose oils with similar benefits that are more suitable for your skin.

- Burn the dried herb Sage throughout your home. Dry out a clump of Sage and bind it with some cotton. Light it so that it is smoking like incense and use the smoke to 'smudge' your house or energy field. Wave the smoke into every corner of your home or around your body using a bowl underneath the Sage stick to catch any ash. This method of cleansing removes heavy layers of negativity. You may wish to combine other herbs with the Sage; use your intuition as to the ones you require. You can also cleanse your home with incense that you purchase from shops.

- Washing down the walls and floors in your home with diluted Eucalyptus oil, Tea Tree and Lemon or Lavender oils will also cleanse the energy in the house. Alternatively you can put these oils into a spray bottle with water and spray the house.

Your intuition may guide you to use different oils or to change the ones you use regularly. Please see the appendix for a list of aromatherapies and suggested spiritual uses if you are unsure of how to begin. Trust your intuition as it knows what is right for you even if the oils do not coincide with the oils suggested in books you may have read, although always be mindful of any contrary indications mentioned. Books can be a helpful way to build your foundation of knowledge in the area of aromatherapy and herbs.

CHAPTER FIVE

The Galactic Level of The Hierarchy

THE SPIRITUAL HIERARCHY FOR EARTH:

The 'etheric' is a term we use to describe the levels connected to Earth that extend beyond Earth and into the outer atmospheres that allow us to connect into the consciousness of humanity. The 'Galactic Levels' is the term we give to etheric levels that are so far beyond Earth that they are more connected to stars and other planetary realms than they are to Earth. The Galactic Levels vibrate within the frequency range of the fourth dimension. It is not until the Upper Galactic Level that the etheric realm becomes fifth dimensional. Because it is difficult for the mind to grasp the immenseness of the galaxy, the following definitions might help to anchor understanding.

Galaxy – 'Any of a vast number of star systems held together by gravitational attraction in an asymmetric shape, or more usually a symmetrical shape, which is either a spiral or an ellipse.'

Galactic plane – 'The plane passing through the spiral arms of the Galaxy.'

Galactic circle – 'The great circle on the celestial sphere containing the galactic plane.' [1]

Contained within the Galactic Levels are the Planetary Councils and Galactic Councils, Council of Twelve, Council of the Mothership and Council of the Directorship of the Rays. These are but a few councils found in the Galactic

---

1. *Collins English Dictionary,* (Harper Collins Publishers, Glasgow Great Brittan, 2003)

Levels and we mention these councils rather than others because they directly relate to an initiate's life on Earth.

Planetary Councils

The two green 'wings' either side with the blue and yellow, red and yellow and light blue and purple triangular structures are representations of the Planetary Councils. Inside these structures are the memory banks of the Soul's experiences within the different planetary civilisations. In this area you will find your past life memory banks of experiences you have had on Earth at different times. Because this area is the planetary consciousness, any experiences your Soul has had on other planetary worlds are also contained here. Many Human Incarnates access their Pleiadian, Sirian, and Learian memory banks here and use these memories to develop and enrich their lives on Earth. (The names Pleiadian, Sirian and Learian are titles given to beings that populate other planetary worlds, for example, the Earthlings of Earth, the Sirians of Sirius, the Learians of Learia and the Pleiadians of the Pleiadies.)

The Galactic Councils

The Galactic Councils depend heavily on the planetary level, where all past experiences and memory banks are stored, to make decisions for the Galactic Level of the Hierarchy. It is in the Core Galactic Council that all Hierarchies, including your own, congregate for the purpose of communicating in a structured and unified way. Many of the decisions affecting the Spiritual Hierarchy for Earth and other Hierarchies in the galaxy are made in these councils. Mandatory council meetings are held regularly in the Galactic Council level where your Hierarchy meets with other Hierarchies. Before and after a major crisis on Earth, all Hierarchies are required to meet at the Galactic Council Level to discuss matters. This is a responsibility each Hierarchy has as being part of the Spiritual Family.

Being consciously connected to the Galactic Council has many benefits in assisting the Human Incarnate to understand the various occurrences on Earth. It is from this council that the Human Incarnate receives the overview or higher perspective on the unfolding of events on Earth. Incarnates can request from this council, a basic understanding of the Earth's blueprint and how they individually can contribute to Earth's highest good. This request can be made by entering into the Hierarchy through the Hierarchy meditation, travelling up in the elevator and asking to stop at the level of the Galactic Council. Once inside the Galactic Council, ask the members for information on your individual contribution to the highest plan for Earth's healing now, or that to which you may aspire in the future.

The Council of Twelve

The Council of Twelve sits just above the Galactic Councils and is represented as the two light blue shields connecting to the flame in the centre of the Hierarchy. This council holds many keys to awareness, spiritual confidence and security. The 'twelve' are the twelve major extensions of your soul and can be seen as the twelve elders of your Hierarchy. When you connect to this level you begin grounding, harmonising and unifying the wisdom, experience and technology of the twelve elders into your human body. Initiates who have reached this level of their Hierarchy are generally drawn to intense periods of meditation, contemplation and peaceful surroundings as they integrate this high level of awareness. They may have one or more out of the twelve elders come to them as a spirit guide to coach them through the phase of integration. It is at this stage of spiritual development that the initiate becomes more intimately aware of who he/she is at a spiritual level. He embraces a level of the spiritual Master within in its feminine and masculine form and comes to integrate the twelve faces or manifestations of this Master.

> **Author's Notes:** Below is a list of twelve elders or categories of representatives that sit on the Council of Twelve. This information has been compiled from my own experience. I sense that all Hierarchies follow a similar blueprint. Please take this example only as a possibility and cross reference it with your own experience as you enter into your own Council of Twelve during meditation. I am drawn to list these possibilities or examples for the purpose of triggering your memories of your own Council or clarifying further the purpose of the Council of Twelve in general. (It is interesting to note the recurrence of 'twelve' as a significant number in spiritual development.)

The Council of Twelve – an example:
1. The Lord and Lady or Masters responsible for holding the Christ Consciousness in the Hierarchy.
2. The Lord and Lady representing the Oceanic consciousness of the Hierarchy.
3. The Angelic Being in its masculine and feminine form representing the Angelic Realm for the Hierarchy.
4. The Lord and Lady representing the Elemental Kingdoms for the Hierarchy.
5. The Lord and Lady representing the Sirian High Council for the Hierarchy.
6. The God and Goddess of the Galactic Plane for the Hierarchy.
7. The masculine and feminine balance of the Ray Being of the Hierarchy.
8. The masculine and feminine balance of the geometry of the Hierarchy.
9. The masculine and feminine balance of the sound of the Hierarchy.
10. The masculine and feminine balance of the light of the Hierarchy.
11. The Ancient Mother of the Hierarchy
12. The Ancient Father of the Hierarchy.

Every now and again Human Incarnates wake in the morning and feel as though they have answers and information that they need for the next phase of their lives. Often they have just spent the night in the Council of Twelve. Although this is an ongoing process that may take a long time, just beginning this process will give you an amazing sense of yourself at a very deep and multidimensional level. Even more beautiful, however, are the waves of self-love and acceptance that begin to wash over you.

Open communication channels to your Council of Twelve by affirming your intention to connect and communicate. You will find it deeply healing and inspiring as you begin this process of setting your intention to connect and watching it manifest. You may wish to use the affirmation:

> *"I allow myself to develop a strong and conscious connection to my Council of Twelve."*

As you affirm this statement of intention close your eyes and feel this intention reaching the council. Feel the Higher Council beginning to connect into your crown as though answering your request.

The Council of The Mothership

THE SPIRITUAL HIERARCHY FOR EARTH:

The next level in the Hierarchy is the Council of the Mothership. Unlike the other councils, the Council of the Mothership transports itself in and out of the Hierarchy. In situations of crisis in the world, Motherships move to areas of the world that need healing and aid. The Mothership is an etheric structure; however those with sight can see the structure of it above areas in the world, while others can sense it. When you are sleeping you have the ability to leave your body and go directly into the Mothership. Spiritual surgery and counselling is often done in Motherships as many Angelic Beings and healing energies work from within the ships. The ships can be considered transportable healing houses. Everything a person could possibly need in order to be healed on a spiritual, emotional and mental level is contained within this ship of healing.

Beings of Light such as Mother Mary, saints and angels work out of the Motherships when they wish to concentrate their healing energies on specific areas in the world. They are able to leave the ships and project their energy into Earth to be of direct assistance when needed. The Mothership allows the Beings of Light to have direct contact with humanity in times of hardship where the energies are dense. You may ask why the Beings of Light would require a ship to reach Earth when they could simply project themselves down. The Mothership can penetrate very dense places stricken with war and conflict. It creates a buffer zone for the Beings of Light to work in without them having to lower their own frequencies in order to work with humanity.

The Council of the Directorship of the Rays

THE ASCENDED MASTER SANAT KUMARA:

The Council of the Directorship of the Rays has twelve members and sits in the middle of your Mothership structure. Like the Mothership this council is fully transportable. Being transportable, the council can direct rays of light and healing technology to any area or group of people in the world. This Council works directly with the 'Ray Being' level which sits above it. I, Sanat Kumara am one of a Council of Twelve that is the Council of the Directorship of the Rays. We are the council that determines the intensity of the ray vibration we direct into different planes and dimensions. The Ray Beings allow their energies to come down through our council and into Earth's atmospheres to reach humanity. Each ray has a different purpose and ability, however they all hold the universal consciousness of masculine/feminine balance and oneness within them.

Each council member of the Directorship of the Rays connects to different aspects of the consciousness of the Earth. Each councillor takes the responsibility of ensuring that they direct the ray energies into the part of the consciousness to which they are connected. They hold the ray's vibrational frequency within them on all planes of creation. They determine the intensity of the ray energy that needs to be released into the plane and its consciousness that they oversee.

Every person on Earth's floor has the ability to connect to at least one council member to receive rays for healing, transformation and evolution. As you ascend upwardly, your connection with the council will strengthen.

CHAPTER SIX

The Upper Galactic Level of The Hierarchy

The Fifth Dimension

The Spiritual Hierarchy for Earth:

Where the fourth dimension has housed the Human Kingdom and has been a workshop for Human Incarnates to resolve their issues and reconnect to their spiritual selves, the fifth dimension is the Spiritual Kingdom. By the time the initiate reaches this kingdom, he/she is already well aware of the purpose of his incarnation, and to a certain extent, the meaning of his life.

The doorway to Christ Consciousness, the fifth dimension is the home base of love. It is a dimension that does not carry the duality of love and fear as the fourth dimension does. It is founded on love and light and as a result many initiates in the upper levels of the fourth dimension aspire to attain fifth dimensional consciousness.

Christ Consciousness

In the early stages of the fifth dimension the initiate is trained by a Christ Consciousness representative to hold the higher frequencies required in fifth dimensional living. A Christ Consciousness representative is any Master or Being of Light who has attained Christ Consciousness and works in the Higher Realms in divine service to Earth and humanity (see The Spiritual Family Chapter Fifteen - Christ Consciousness Companion).

The initiate then trains to work as an Ascended Master upon Earth's floor and uses his developing relationship and communication with his Hierarchy to assist him. He works as an emissary for his Hierarchy on the physical plane. He recognises his role within the Spiritual Hierarchy for Earth and his place within his own Hierarchy. He works as Divine Will in Action as part of his service to the planet and humanity.

The Sun Level

The Sun Level marks the doorway into the Fifth Dimension and the Upper Galactic Level of the Hierarchy. The Sun Level holds a unique energy for the Hierarchy, like sunlight does for the Earth. The energy promotes growth and sends an endless source of inspiration and motivation into all parts of the Hierarchy. Christ Consciousness and the Christ Consciousness Higher Council hold offices in the Sun Level of all Hierarchies and provide a training and initiation doorway into the Universal levels of the Hierarchy. Until one can hold the energy of the Sun level and integrate it into life on Earth, one cannot ascend 100 percent into the universal levels of Oneness. The Sun Level is the attainment of Christ Consciousness or the awareness of the Oneness of all things. The Sun level can be a euphoric experience and a taste of what life will be like for everyone when humanity is fully integrated in this energy and we as a Global/Spiritual Family all live in Christ Consciousness together.

Strengthening Your Connection to the Sun Level and Christ Consciousness

- Sit comfortably in a warm and supportive environment (you may wish to be where you can feel the sun itself).
- Close your eyes and breathe.
- Feel that right above you, high, high above you there is a warm sun.
- You can feel the warm glow of its golden, orange and yellow light on your face.
- It travels down every level of your Hierarchy towards you.

- As it moves closer to your physical body it penetrates the layers of your energy field.
- Its light is so pure and loving that it transmutes any negativity around or within you.
- You can feel it penetrating your emotional body. You start to feel warmer, and more loving.
- Your body releases any rigidity and tension effortlessly.
- The warm light continually moves through you in waves and your heart responds and begins to open.
- The Golden Light of the Christ Consciousness enters into your heart.
- Feelings of kindness, empathy and compassion come to the surface. The limitations of the past disappear.
- Your heart reaches forgiveness and complete openness with the Christ Consciousness warmth around you.
- You stay for a while in this divine light and then you return slowly and open your eyes.

The Sixth Dimension

In the sixth dimension, the divine initiate leaves behind what remains of his understanding of separateness and prepares to immerse himself in the knowing of the Oneness of God. He recognises the truth of God and understands God to be the Force of Light, the Source of Light, the Oneness, the All that Is. He surrenders his limitations about how he perceives himself and he moves into the realm of unlimited possibility. It is here that he ceases to know himself as the physical Incarnated Self and comes to know himself as the All that Is. It is here he attains the complete surrender of Self into the All that Is. He becomes all things from the rocks to the birds to the stars and planets. He attains God Consciousness.

The Shambhala Council

The Shambhala Council vibrates in the same frequency range as the sixth dimension. The Shambhala Council is both at this level and in the core of the Earth, which is not represented on this particular structure. The Shambhala Council consists of Ancient Beings that were on the council prior to the creation of Earth. These beings oversee the Earth, yet do not interfere or directly influence any Earth decisions made in the councils below. The Shambhala energy is the Direct Will of God, and thus to ascend into the Universal levels, one is required to be in complete alignment with this energy in order to resonate with the Universal Frequencies.

When integrating this level, your human/physical body may begin to shift in a new way, awakening new levels of inner power. In the Shambhala level, a new sense of self-empowerment activates as a result of being more deeply aligned to the Will of God. You may experience shifts mentally and in your relationships as energies in your life readjust to the new alignment.

Connecting with the Shambhala Level

For those familiar with the Chakras (powerful energy systems/spinning centres of light in the body), you will find that developing the Shambhala level deeply shifts the Hara system. The Hara region is below the navel and is not one point but an area of light. The Hara is a template for higher consciousness in the human body. Within this template are codes for living in a higher state of alignment to the Divine Will as well as doorways to other dimensions. By focusing on the Hara in meditation you can travel through the Hara and discover inter-dimensional doorways to Higher Realms and levels of consciousness. Meditate on this whole region below your navel and feel aligned to the Shambhala Councils, both above you and below you, with your physical and energetic bodies.

CHAPTER SEVEN

The Universal Level of The Hierarchy

The Seventh Dimension

THE SPIRITUAL HIERARCHY FOR EARTH:

Referred to as 'Seventh Heaven', the seventh dimension is home to many Angelic and Celestial Beings as well as the Universal Levels of the Hierarchy.

Once the Master has surrendered to the releasing of himself into the All that Is of the sixth dimension, he may elect to gather himself again into a form of his choosing and rejoin the Community of Light within the seventh dimension. As he reaches the seventh dimension, many options are presented to him. He may choose to be of service to Earth and humanity or may work on other planetary worlds and realms different to Earth. He is given the option to manifest himself within the many different forms of his Hierarchy and can shape-shift to appear as he wishes to. He may choose to manifest at any given time as the wind, the rain, the water, a bird, animal or fish. This shape-shifting is always done with the permission of others involved. He may also choose to manifest himself as a Ray Being, one possible manifestation of his Universal Self.

If he chooses to come back and work for the Spiritual Hierarchy for Earth, he is aligned to an assignment. This assignment is designed by himself and the overseeing board of the Spiritual Hierarchy for Earth.

In the seventh dimension the Master has access to his full Co-Creational

Self. The Master has the ability to connect to a new level of initiation whereby he undertakes awakening into his full Creator God self. He comes to realise himself not only as All Things but as an aspect of the Creator of All Things. As he comes to understand this he begins to manifest himself as the Creator and takes his place within the Office of God. This sees him training as an aspect of God and here he undergoes initiation to take this Mantle of Light, Greatness and Wisdom. He takes his seat at the round table in the Office of God.

The Ray Being Level

The Ray Being level is part of the Universal level and is connected to the Soul level, the highest part of the Hierarchy. The Ray Being is a manifestation of the Universal Consciousness and because it is at a very high level of the Hierarchy, represents purity and Oneness Consciousness. This level is free of karmic contracts and duality and is the Oneness that many seek. The Ray Being energies flow down through the frequencies into the many levels of life on Earth's floor. The Ray Beings are part of a complex system that determines the distribution of the ray energies and vibrations.

The Universal Level

The Rays or Ray Beings are in fact Beings of Light in their own right. They live at the Universal Level of a Hierarchy. These beings have a unique consciousness that comes together with other parts of the consciousness (other Ray Beings) to create the Universal Consciousness. Each person on Earth belongs to a Ray Group which is the extension of a Ray Being. A Ray Group is all aspects of one's Hierarchy that hold the same vibration as their higher aspect (the Ray Being).

Each and every person on Earth's floor is a member of a Hierarchy and are thus a shard of light from the Ray Being.

The Soul Level

While your Hierarchy ceases to be in the form of a Hierarchy structure beyond the Ray Being level, here the structure takes on a new form and becomes the geometry of the Soul itself. This is called the Soul Level. Even though in truth all things are One, within the Hierarchy, your essence may experience itself as individual aspects, just as you experience differences between yourself and other people. At the Soul level, separateness and individuality ceases to be and all things come home to the Oneness. Because the essence no longer wishes to experience its individual aspects, the Hierarchy has no purpose and thus ceases to hold its form at the Universal Level. As you progress up into the Universal Level, towards the Soul Level, the residual separateness from the Hierarchy experience dissolves until, within the Soul Level, all things merge into Oneness, the All that Is, the universal life force without manifestation into specific form.

What to Expect as Your Awareness Expands

We have now discussed with you each relevant level of your Hierarchy and how these relate to your personal and spiritual development. The structure diagram that you have been looking at triggers the memory banks in you so that you can more deeply remember these other levels. Through this conscious awareness, the process can be accelerated while minimising the pain and discomfort often experienced by not understanding. The process of reconnecting will see many different body shifts, cleanses and realignments. Your sleeping patterns may alter and change regularly. You may have strange days where you are not quite sure what dimension you are actually in, and emotionally and mentally you will systematically release old energies to make way for higher vibrations.

It gets easier and easier the higher up you move and the more you integrate the levels you ascend into (either because as an incarnate you become used to it, or it does actually become easier!) There is a rhythm and a flow to the reconnection process. The more you let go and allow, the sooner you move more gracefully into the cycles. There is, most importantly, a deeper sense of peace, love and wisdom that integrates within and although ever changing, this sense of serenity becomes a consistent experience and reality.

The relationship with your Hierarchy develops and strengthens as you work consciously to reconnect to the support it gives you. We suggest consistent use of the 'Consciously Connecting to your Hierarchy' meditation at the end of Chapter 1. What we give you is a foundational tool, however you will alter it as you work with it and adapt it to best serve your needs.

CHAPTER EIGHT

Understanding Incarnation

ST GERMAIN:

An aspect of your Hierarchy has many functions as a result of choosing to come to Earth as a Human Incarnate. Before he/she is even able to manifest in human form, there is an in-depth procedure that must be carried out. The role and position of the Human Incarnate must be agreed upon by the Higher Council of Higher Self, and in some cases, where it requires assistance from other Hierarchies, at the meetings of the Galactic Councils. An aspect of the Hierarchy's spirit is not allowed to manifest itself whimsically. There is a careful selection procedure to determine the right aspect of the Hierarchy for the job. There is also a meticulous planning procedure as is explained in the 'Incarnation Council' where the exact circumstances of the birth and environment is pre-ordained. Commonly there are three ways that an aspect will become a Human Incarnate.

The First Way – The Aspect Requests the Opportunity to Incarnate

The first way as partially indicated above, is where the aspect decides that it wishes to incarnate. At this point it approaches the Incarnation Council and the Higher Council of Higher Self. The aspect's request is considered and if need be, the Hierarchy may seek assistance or advice from other Hierarchies. The Hierarchy will decide whether the aspect's incarnation will ultimately evolve and assist the evolution of the individual aspect as well as the Hierarchy and All That Is. Even those incarnations that you may judge as 'bad', where the human is conducting him/herself in a disruptive or inhumane way, may be decided upon as ultimately beneficial for the Hierarchy and All That Is.

In situations where the aspect's incarnation request is rejected, the Hierarchy will work to find an arrangement where the aspect's needs and aspirations are still met. An alternative may be to incarnate in a different form, or in a different lifetime. The aspect may also be recommended to incarnate in a different planetary system, or undergo a training and initiation process before incarnating.

Not all applications to incarnate are accepted by the Higher Councils. Many aspects are not always equipped with (a) the desire or (b) the skills required to survive the incarnation process. Some aspects of a Hierarchy may not be trained in incarnation or have had any earthly experience in living in the confines of Earth's current dimensional structure. The structure of the aspect itself may be damaged through an incorrect entry into the physical plane, which may be the result of insufficient training. Entering the physical plane requires the aspect to lower its vibrational frequency in order to fit into the dimensional and frequency limitations of Earth's current geometrical structure and blueprint. Earth is still relatively unevolved in terms of reaching its multidimensional capacity. It can hold multiple frequency bands and the energy to access many dimensional planes of creation. It has not yet, however, evolved to hold high vibrational frequencies where it can permanently open dimensional doorways to allow conscious co-existence between humanity and other star and planetary races.

This means that although Earth is a multidimensional system as yet it is not of the ability to hold the energy and frequencies for full multidimensional expression. For example, a department store may have twenty-four levels and in each level there are many compartments, shops and movie theatres. Earth has only explored the first level of the department store. We still, however, classify Earth as multidimensional for in the first level it has explored many of that level's compartments and has the ability to move beyond the first level itself.

In the case of an aspect's incarnation application being rejected, we use the experiences of a deep-sea diver to explain the reasons. When a diver attempts to dive deeply into the sea, he/she is aware that the further he goes down, the more intense the pressure. He must go down very slowly and come up very slowly and there are certain precautions that must be taken. Incorrect procedure may result in the severe damage or death of the diver. This is the same for an aspect of a Hierarchy desiring to go down from the tenth floor of the department store, for example, to the first floor. We must ensure that the aspect integrates each level as it goes down and once down understand that it cannot always come up again in a hurry.

There are some exceptions to this rule such that some beings can move faster than others, up and down through the frequencies; in fact, some beings specialise in it. The training, experience, capacity to integrate, design and structure of the aspect will determine the speed at which it can move through these levels. Ascended Masters must go through an initiation process as part of their Ascended Master training that entails them to master the ability to move quite quickly through all levels with grace and ease. Many people on Earth's floor are actually in training for this training, and some are already in the Ascended Master training as we speak. Some people already have the training and are simply awakening into it.

A dramatic drop in the frequencies as an aspect incarnates down through the levels is a major reason the incarnation application may be rejected. Other times it is the reverse where the aspect has spent too much time on the physical plane and would benefit more from a higher perspective through integrating many non-physical realms into their experience. As I, St Germain spoke earlier, there are three main ways an aspect may become **a Human Incarnate** and we have now touched on the first way.

The Second Way – The Aspect is Chosen by the Higher Councils. It is Asked to Volunteer

The second way is through the desire of the Council of Twelve, the Higher Council of Higher Self and the Universal Councils. They co-operate to send a representative of the Hierarchy, an aspect, to anchor the force of the Hierarchy, the Hierarchy's full intention and other dimensional frequencies of the Hierarchy, onto Earth's floor. This representative will generally keep in communication with the councils and have a fairly clear understanding of its assignment even when it has entered into human/physical form. This aspect tends to direct, assist and lead many other incarnated aspects of its Hierarchy into new levels of consciousness. It is generally aware of other humans that are incarnated aspects from its own Hierarchy (see diagram 5). It is often aware of each of the different assignments of these aspects.

This aspect may choose to take on the karmic requirements of being a human on Earth, where it is conditioned by the psyche of the world. For example, the aspect will take on many of the belief systems in the mass consciousness such as "I need to protect myself" or, "There is not enough for everyone" etc. It will then complete karma associated with this by releasing the lower vibrations of the psyche of the world caught in its own psyche, thus releasing many of its other aspects already incarnated.

The aspect can take on the karma of other aspects of the Hierarchy that have not incarnated at this point in time and can clear the karma for the whole consciousness and energy of the Hierarchy. This is permitted providing the non-incarnated aspects live in the energy field of the incarnated aspect. The non-incarnated aspect attaches itself to the energy field of the incarnated aspect like a 'spirit guide' would. This allows it to be close to the Earth plane and therefore able to experience what the incarnated aspect is experiencing, while the karma is being cleared. This ensures that the non-incarnated aspect receives the experience of the karma being cleared as well as taking responsibility for the karma created in the first place.

The non-incarnated aspect does not need to physically 'live' in the incarnated aspect while the karma is being cleared, however it is required to vibrate at the same vibrational frequency of the incarnated aspect's energy fields while the karma is being cleared. It is the responsibility of the non-incarnated aspect to direct and assist the incarnated aspect while the karma is being cleared.

The Hierarchy may have many hundreds of aspects that need to clear karma through the non-incarnation process. It is not necessary for all of these to incarnate, particularly if the karma can be cleared, for example, in two days of experience.

The Third Way – The Aspect Recognises it Needs to Clear Karma and Evolve Beyond Dynamics Carried Over from Past Lives

The third way in which an aspect of the Hierarchy may be incarnated is through the aspect's desire at a higher level, to evolve itself into a position where it can take its place within many council seats and realities within its Hierarchy. This aspect may have many levels of past life karma that needs to be released before it can hold the frequencies required in order for it to take its place in council. The aspect may spend years working through its relationship with money, friends, family, work, health and institutions. The aspect may remain relatively unaware of its purpose for being on Earth.

If the aspect chooses to evolve and awaken itself, it will seek to heal relationships with family and friends. It may seek alternative care for health issues or break away from limiting institutionalised ideas that are considered a normal part of society. It may find itself consciously working through challenging dynamics with others in order to clear the karma picked up in past life times. As the human does this, it evolves itself and assists in the evolution of others. Once the aspect has reached this stage, it will automatically draw to itself situations that will deepen its level of self-awareness and compassion.

If the human reaches this far in its development, it may elect (election is done at a higher level – not necessarily a conscious Earth choice) to be initiated into higher levels of awareness. At this point the aspect becomes an initiate and can choose to be initiated into levels of training where it takes on a mantle of higher consciousness and responsibility. This may be to take on one of the assignments outlined in the next chapter.

Always in the Third Way, whether the person elects for further levels of training and roles or not, his greatest achievement is to leave Earth knowing he completed all of his chosen requirements by clearing karma and making peace with himself. This person can evolve himself in the same lifetime from being relatively unaware to being consciously aware in the manner outlined in the Second Way.

CHAPTER NINE

Assignments of the Human Incarnate

Author's Notes: In the previous chapter we explored three ways an aspect of a Hierarchy can incarnate into human form. In this chapter we look at different roles or assignments an aspect may agree to prior to incarnating, or may take on and train for, once he/she has incarnated. As you read through the descriptions of these assignments one or more may jump out and speak to you. You may see yourself in the description, or other people that you know. Although it is by no means the complete picture, you can use this information to deepen your understanding of your purpose on Earth.

ST GERMAIN:

The Torch Bearer

The Torch Bearer holds the flame of Vision. This initiate holds the flame of future possibility. Where there is no hope, the Torch Bearer brings faith. The Torch Bearer holds the torch of light through the times of darkness on Earth and lights the way for others. This person does not lead the way through teaching and/or overly exposing himself to public view for this is not his assignment. The Torch Bearer simply shines the light upon the doorway and leaves it up to each and every individual to walk through the doorway in their own right.

When people cannot lift their heads to see the way clear, the Torch Bearer brings the courage to do so. This is done by presenting the light, the torch of future possibility. In this modern world, the Torch Bearer exists in many different places such as committees, in the corporate arena, and in supportive, caring roles for others. He is the one that presents the innovative ideas of hope and inspiration. He is the one that humbly suggests higher paths to take and options that bring more beneficial outcomes. The Torch Bearer gives hints, nudges and brighter perspectives to those lost in the illusion of little possibility. The Torch Bearer is one who goes quietly about his/her business, inspiring others when called to.

A Torch Bearer does not interfere in another's path, nor tries to convince, teach or lead. The Torch Bearer works more subtly than this; a quiet type, he has an extremely high level of awareness and uses it to supports others.

The Circuit Breaker

The Circuit Breaker focuses on the patterns, cycles and behaviours in the family environment. Generally this person consciously works to transcend damaging and limiting family cycles by studying the family's belief systems. The Circuit Breaker investigates the family consciousness and may look into the past generations of the family. This person will observe her own patterns and beliefs and will seek to transcend them. In transcending her own behaviours she breaks the circuit for future generations. This is so because patterns in families are often repeated if not consciously broken. By saying 'no' to an old family cycle, the power of the cycle and its hold over the family is diminished.

A negative pattern or belief as it is passed down from generation to generation is able to gain more power depending on how much the next generation invests in it. A family pattern and cycle can work like the wheels of a machine, the more they spin the longer it takes for them to come to a complete stop. A Circuit Breaker, as part of her life work, will seek to understand these cycles. Once these cycles are understood they can be controlled. Awareness brings the power back to the individual and then to the family. Once the awareness is attained, action can then take place. The individual or family is empowered to put supportive systems in place to ensure the cycle is not repeated.

For example, Janet traced the abuse of alcohol back through her family. She discovered that her grandfather drank heavily and so did his father. She discovered that they drank for many reasons including the desire to escape from their realities. They both had many children with little income. She knew from personal experience that her grandfather never expressed himself and redirected his need for an outlet into the consumption of alcohol. Janet's mother, the daughter of the grandfather she had been investigating, married Janet's father who also drank. Janet's mother Susan did not directly take on the pattern of her father by drinking; however, by marrying someone that did, she continued the cycle.

Janet knew she could not change the lives of her parents; they had already made their choices. What she wanted to transform was the quality of her own life and that of her children and later, her grandchildren. She knew the only way to do this was to heal herself. She looked at where she had repeated the pattern in her own life. She recognised the use of substances to hide from reality was repeated through her addiction to pharmaceutical drugs such as anti-depressants.

Janet decided to break this pattern and find the underlying cause of her depression. She discovered that she had unresolved anger towards her parents, family in general and the male line right through her family. She worked with a counsellor, her own journal writing, meditation, books and a healing circle of like minded friends, to resolve her anger. She took her power back from the situation and then forgave it. She did not try to 'fix' anyone else, but chose instead to heal herself. Janet transcended the pattern and as a result broke a circuit that may have continued to infiltrate generations to come. By taking responsibility and working with forgiveness, she healed herself and the future for her children.

Circuit Breakers are jewels of great light to the world. They understand that if the community is a tree, the family is the trunk. They understand that branches cannot grow properly if the trunk is not strong. Circuit Breakers seek to strengthen the trunk.

The Way-Shower

The Way-Shower is a person prepared to 'go out on a limb' in order to improve his/her life and contribute to the world. This person is prepared to take risks regardless of the judgement he may receive from others. Over

Earth's history, some Way-Showers have been persecuted, jailed and in some cases put to death. The Way-Shower is aligned to the divine plan and works directly with the Angels and Beings of Light. He may not always be fully conscious of this connection or his purpose on Earth but has a strong sense of justice and personal integrity.

Way-Showers work in many areas on Earth. Some Way-Showers work in politics, humanitarian and environmental organisations and community groups. There are some Way-Showers however, that have family roles rather than roles in the wider world. These people show the way to members of the family by setting a higher example of living. Such Way-Showers may embark upon their spiritual paths and as a result transform their lives. This living example shows the way to family and friends.

A person who is a Way-Shower in his family can also be a Circuit Breaker. A Way-Shower is a person that clears the debris away from the path. This person cuts away the dead branches and bracken to make a clear path for others to follow. He walks the path he has cleared and others often follow along behind him as he steps into a higher frequency. A Way-Shower is a leader by example.

The Light-Worker

When looking at the role of a Light-Worker it is necessary to revisit Chapter Eight. Whether a person is a Light-Worker before he/she incarnates, or trains to become one during incarnation, depends on the way he/she incarnated. In the Second Way, the initiate already bears the title of Light-Worker before she incarnates. In the Third Way, the Human Incarnate, having chosen to awaken to a higher level of her spiritual process, trains to attain the title and role of a Light-Worker, partly by embodying the principles of a Light-Worker whilst living her everyday life. A Light-Worker is a person who is aligned to the highest plan for Earth. The person works consciously to assist humanity and Earth to realise this divine plan.

Light-Worker training goes hand in hand with the Ascension process. The function of the training is to assist the initiate to be consciously aware of her assignments and purpose on Earth. It is to teach her to channel divine love and light on a day to day basis in every situation. The Light-Worker is required and will be tested to attain levels of compassion, empathy, care and consideration for all living things. The Light-Worker is required to understand the equality of all things and to work in harmony with the natural cycles and divine plan of Earth.

It is important to note that an individual may hold more than one role and assignment at the same time, for example a Light-Worker and a Way-Shower.

CHAPTER TEN

Exploring Ascension

The Ascension Process

SPIRITUAL HIERARCHY FOR EARTH:

In the Ascension process the Human Incarnate awakens to the fact that he is on a spiritual path and then consciously works to understand his path by attaining higher levels of awareness. This process unfolds differently for each individual but the underlying principles are the same. Many Human Incarnates start their journey unconsciously by searching for ways to heal themselves, to resolve issues that keep reappearing in their lives and to find fulfilment and inspiration.

To assist in the Ascension process, the Higher Self encourages the initiate to seek deeper and deeper knowledge both internally and externally as a way of activating the Ascension blueprint within his physical body. The Ascension blueprint is the body's cellular program or 'instruction manual' on how to move the Human Incarnate into higher states of awareness. The Ascension blueprint lives inside the blueprint of the human body. The Ascension process is broken down into levels. The Human Incarnate systematically ascends through each level, which can take many years. Once the initiate reaches the dimension he desires, he may rest at that level before continuing on in his Ascension process when he is ready for the next phase of his journey.

When he ascends he moves from a third dimensional energy and framework into the fifth dimension which is the Gateway of the Christ Consciousness. The fourth dimension is the transitional plane that assists him to integrate the principles of Christ Consciousness and taste many of its frequencies before entering completely into the power, intensity and love of this energy. Once he/she has entered into the fifth dimension, he automatically has the opportunity to continue on ascending into the sixth and seventh dimensions. He may decide however, to make the fifth dimension his home and still connect to the sixth and seventh energetically. Once the initiate has entered into the fifth dimension, he is an aspect of his multidimensional self and experiences the freedom of moving freely and gracefully through the dimensional planes and frequencies.

Those who incarnate through the First Way may, or may not, do so with the intention of Ascending. Their Ascension process may begin automatically as was agreed prior to their incarnation, or they may decide to do so as their life unfolds.

In the Second Way, explained in the previous chapter, the Ascension process begins automatically. This is because the initiate agrees to wear the veils of non-remembering for a certain time to understand Earth and humanity, but as soon as this information is adequately processed the veils come off and Ascension begins.

In the Third Way, Ascension begins through agreement. The person begins to leave his body at night time and travels into his Higher Councils. Here he has many discussions about his possibilities and is supported in his choice to Ascend. His choice to Ascend was most likely made before his incarnation. The meetings in the councils at night simply reaffirm this choice and give the council permission to prepare him for the Ascension phase. Once the preparations have been made he is ready to embark upon his journey, the Ascension Process. Ascension begins when the blueprint that exists within the human body activates a new level of itself and signals that it is now time to awaken.

Earth Assignments – Activating the Blueprint

Once a person has incarnated on Earth's floor, regardless of the incarnation process chosen, he will begin immediately moving through each of the assignments outlined in his blueprint (for blueprint see Definitions section). The human being, although not generally consciously aware, knows at an innate level, what direction he needs to move in, in order to fulfil his self-created requirements. In childhood he begins to acquire the information and training that he will need later on in life. The parents that he has chosen unconsciously supply all information and lessons that are needed.

The blueprint of each and every individual is encoded into the cellular structure and memory of the human body. Levels of the blueprint activate as the individual reaches stages in life where the next level of encoded information is required. One basic example of this is when a person is in a job and then wakes up with or moves into a growing desire to change occupations. The occupation was very fulfilling in the past, but as the new phase begins, it no longer satisfies her. This growing desire comes from the new level of the blueprint that has activated.

When a person tries to resist the inevitable and natural flow of moving into the next stage of fulfilling her blueprint, she becomes uncomfortable and finds that 'nothing seems to be working'. The Hierarchy uses frustration as a motivational energy to urge their Human Incarnate to start moving in the right direction. Dissatisfaction with life can also be an indicator that the incarnate hasn't quite embraced the new levels of her blueprint and thus feels a lack of fulfilment with her current circumstances. In some cases, to move into the next level of the blueprint does not always require radical changes; it may simply call for a shift in perspective or to start a project that has been put off.

Often an incarnate is fearful of new stages of her blueprint even though innately she knows that it holds the keys to her creative power and fulfilment. She experiences fear as she realises that changes in belief systems and behaviours need to be made in order for her to come into full empowerment. She realises that her power in its pure and true form, allows her to recognise levels of her greatness. It is this greatness that often intimidates humanity in general because it brings with it an awareness that allows humanity to know, recognise and fulfil its Oneness with God. It is this God energy that humanity has put outside itself for many centuries and is now being encouraged to recognise within.

What creates the fear in humanity is the centuries of very deeply embedded misconceptions encoded into the global unconscious about power. Power in its true and pure form is a very useful and constructive force. It has been the misuse of lower levels of power that has led humanity to believe that this force is a dangerous one and better left in God's hands. The shift in consciousness now occurring within humanity is that this true power is a divine force to be loved, trusted and appreciated.

First Stage of Ascension – The Initial Awakening

Once an incarnate decides to embrace this fear of power, greatness and God, and to move toward embracing his inner power, the blueprint begins to activate even more deeply and intensely. The rush of desire for self-discovery and self-understanding activates in the Body Cell Memory (see the Definitions section) and moves through the energy centres and fields enticing the incarnate to seek information and opportunity for awakening. A person, who may not have previously been overly concerned with spiritual development, begins to read metaphysical material, attend workshops of a spiritual basis, and seek the counsel of those already involved in stages of their awakening process. Sometimes a person may not be consciously aware of this awakening procedure and thus will unconsciously manifest spiritual books as gifts or meet certain people who have information about the process.

Once the incarnate begins to awaken he gradually becomes aware of aspects of himself that he wants to change. He recognises a need to heal parts of himself that are angry, irresponsible, depressed, unco-operative, and self-sabotaging. He directly or indirectly requests assistance from others or 'higher powers' to shift damaging behaviours and will find himself seeking and listening to alternatives. He may become aware of his Hierarchy or at least higher energies through dreams, thoughts and experiences that may have a profound influence. He senses that he is not alone and that there may be a higher purpose to being on Earth's floor. Gradually he shifts from conducting himself in a relatively unconscious way, to becoming aware of thoughts, feelings and actions. After an initial stage of confusion as the new level of the blueprint activates, things start to make sense and the past forms a clearer picture. The individual can sense that all things that occurred in the past were essential in terms of bringing him to his current position of awakening.

The process advances to the point where the incarnate starts to realise the full power and potential of his current choices. He takes conscious steps forward, understanding and taking responsibility for all choices made. This responsibility, he finds, is actually liberating as it brings with it a sense of freedom and clarity. Less and less he creates situations of pain, suffering and chaos. More and more his choices bring abundance, creative manifestation and happiness. It is at this point that he begins to view life and himself from a different perspective.

In areas where he has either given his power away, or has tried to assert power over others, he balances the energy, creating healthier, happier dynamics with others. The incarnate gradually moves away from situations that are damaging or destructive.

Relationships of a co-dependent nature often break down or transcend as the Human Incarnate progresses along the Ascension path. From this, the incarnate begins to create new relationships or transform the current relationship dynamic so that it is based on a foundation of personal integrity. Self-worth, value and appreciation comes into the equation as the person begins to view himself differently and thus begins to appreciate others more deeply. He realises that as he hurts others, he hurts himself and vice versa. All of these revelations are essential elements within the awakening procedure and although each person will experience each stage differently, they will still come to the same understanding.

If the incarnate has not already done so, he will move into his true life work either during or after this stage of awareness. This transition can take many years to complete. The life work is compatible with the person's new stage of awakening and will allow the room to continue the self-discovery process. The incarnate will find that in some way, his experiences on the road of self-discovery are used to assist, educate or understand others.

Regardless of the occupation, the life work of the incarnate will ultimately benefit humanity and the world. Even though there will be challenges or opportunities for further growth and expansion, he will experience deep satisfaction and certainty from his work and will feel passionate and motivated again. Other areas of his life benefit from the creative energy that activates in the body and energy field with the Ascension process. New projects will begin, others will be completed and new life, colour, sound and vibrant energy revitalise all areas of his life.

It is a wonderful phase of a person's spiritual awakening and from our point of view, a wonderful one to watch and observe. We feel excited to witness you beginning to understand the perfection and creative potential of life. This is similar to a mother watching her child realise his potential when he discovers he has a nose to breathe through, legs to walk on, and fingers with which to clutch things.

The Second Stage of Ascension – Discovering the Multidimensional Self

There are stages after the initial awakening phase where the person begins to take his spiritual power and come into the spiritual maturity of his being. It is at this stage that the incarnate begins to manifest his higher potential on to the physical plane. He realises, at least in theory, that he is an aspect of the whole, of the Oneness of All that Is. He awakens to the understanding that with a connection to the rest of the Hierarchy, he can truly experience himself as whole. The incarnate reconnects with his Higher Mind/Higher Self and moves into conscious awareness of his multidimensional form.

This multidimensional awareness opens up as he recalls the work and travel he does at night while sleeping. The sleeping period is used by the Hierarchy to call the incarnate home to realms and levels within the Hierarchy, including council meetings and discussions. Gradually the incarnate begins to remember these council meetings when he wakes up in the morning. He realises that he exists in other time/space matrices other than the Earth frequencies. He may also recognise that he doesn't always manifest as a human form in other dimensions and thus realises his capacity to be all things. The incarnate begins to understand that he has an instrumental role in not only his own life-plan, but the decision-making process for Earth and humanity. He realises that there is a definite higher procedure by which everyone is connected and forms a part thereof. It is this level of understanding that brings yet another level of self-responsibility and spiritual maturity.

The Third Stage of Ascension – Training Within the Frequencies

In the Third Stage of Ascension the incarnate enters a series of initiations and training programs designed by the Hierarchy. These programs change the vibrational frequency of the initiate so that he has the capacity to hold higher sets of frequencies simultaneously. This Third Phase accelerates dramatically the initiate's spiritual development as it not only trains him to consciously hold the frequencies, but also allows access to the wisdom and technology contained within the frequency. Traditionally this process has been known as 'Discovering the Mysteries'; having sacred mysteries revealed through spiritual initiation. Mysteries are revealed as the initiate demonstrates his ability to hold the energy for and of the mystery, and the ability to integrate the wisdom contained within the information. As in all three phases, Ascension is the initiate's progression through the frequency bands. The initiate moves from a relatively low vibrational set of frequencies to a higher vibrational set of frequencies and a higher amount of frequencies contained in the sets themselves.

A frequency exists within a geometrical structure that is created through the frequency's vibrational capacity. Contained within the frequency itself is information, which can manifest in the form of light, colour and sound. The level of information that can be stored in a frequency is determined by the frequency's geometric structure, which is created by the frequency's vibrational capacity. The third phase of training within the frequencies will assist the initiate to transform his limiting perceptions about reality into a more universal understanding.

A Rare Phenomenon that can Occur in the Third Phase

There is a rare phenomenon that can occur in some initiates when the intergalactic memory banks activate in the cells as the blueprint activates. The initiate may for some time perceive the universe and all contained within it as a series of scientific/mathematical formulas. He begins to realise that everything in the universe is a geometrical and mathematical structure and may for a while read the geometrical blueprint of a situation rather than its physical manifestation. Not all initiates will or need to experience this phenomenon. Often initiates may have an inkling that the universe is made up of mathematical formulas, but decide not to travel too far into that area. Even those that do will do so in varying degrees. The more scientifically, geometrically or mathematically interested the initiate is, the stronger his desire to explore this level.

Although there are many similarities, the science we speak of is not precisely the same as science learnt in the institutions on Earth's floor. The science, found particularly at the Galactic Levels of a Hierarchy, recognises that everything is a formula. Every emotion, thought, feeling and creation is a series of scientific, mathematical equations. The initiate realises that he can change his thoughts, feelings or emotions by finding the correct formula. He begins to write down on paper, numbers, designs and words that may not make a lot of sense to the human mind. Sacred writings and symbols flow through his pen, and he realises that in some way, these writings are having a beneficial effect. The initiate has tapped into the sacred language of the universe. As his eyes scan this sacred language, it activates levels of his body cell memory and blueprint responsible for healing and awakening. Guides and spiritual Masters of a geometric, scientific and mathematical vibration move closer and train him to learn and understand more in this area.

Not all initiates are ready, nor desire to go quite this far into the exploration of the universe as formulas. An initiate can lose himself through experiencing Earth, all of its realms and the universe as a scientific formula. The initiate can cease to see reality as his fellow brothers and sisters of Earth do and can be lost to those around him. He may be unable to hold the level of awareness required for a balanced earthly life and may find himself in dimensional experiences not compatible with his current earthly life.

Regardless of how far the initiate travels into this area, he will come through the 'tunnel' and out the other side. It is here he will hold the memory of his experiences, integrate them into his earthly life and them resume the creation of his life on Earth. In time he will 'return', bring his experiences back with him and live life with greater awareness. This is what we call the integration of this phase.

There are immense benefits to this level of exploration as the initiate has the opportunity to transcend his illusions of the Earth plane. Instead of believing that Earth dictates reality to him, he realises that he projects his view onto Earth thus creating his view as reality. The initiate learns that as his perceptions change, his experience of Earth and human beings change. He learns that whole realities can alter through the alteration of the formulas by which they are created. The initiate understands the delicate nature of the universe and the perfection of creation. He understands that he does in fact create his experience; as he perceives, so does he experience.

Generally speaking, the initiate who takes this path to its fullest, to its final test, is in search of the highest truth. As he systematically pulls back the layers, he finds many levels of truth, but rest assured, he will come to absolute truth and this shall be his liberation.

In the Third Phase, whether the initiate moves deeply into the scientific aspects or not, he will learn about receiving higher energies, grounding these into his human body, into the core of the Earth, and then integrating these energies into life on Earth. The initiate understands one of his roles on Earth's floor is being a vessel in which to receive higher energies. He holds the energies in his human body and allows them to emanate from him, thus raising the vibration of humanity as a whole. Through this method he is giving those within his vicinity the opportunity to benefit directly from these vibrations.

It is in this way that each and every person on Earth's floor can become a healer and Ascended Master. All have the ability to connect to higher energies and then anchor these energies into humanity. As each individual takes responsibility for this part of their role on Earth's floor, humanity shall elevate itself into a consistent higher state, thus experiencing itself as Ascended on Earth's floor.

Tools and Techniques to Assist in Ascension

There are certain tools and techniques that you can incorporate into your spiritual life that can assist you in your Ascension. Focusing on Light is definitely the strongest technique as Ascension is about transforming the physical self with Light and becoming Light. Drawing the Light into your body, mind and energy fields every day is most effective and can be done through meditation, breathing techniques, focusing on the sun, being aware of the healing benefits of sunlight and thinking 'light' thoughts.

'Aspect Therapy' is a profound way of clearing away blockages that prevent you from ascending. Aspect Therapy is discussed in full detail later on in the text (refer to Chapter 12).

Alongside Aspect Therapy, fresh air, physical exercise, and eating nurturing, healthy foods are definitely on our list. These things support the physical body that needs your love and nurturing through this time of transformation. The body requires its physical needs be met before it will venture into new lands. It will 'read' the amount of support it is getting from you and will use this information to decide how quickly it can move itself. The physical body burns a lot of fuel as it prepares to Ascend and thus requires that it be fed well.

Many people believe that little food is beneficial. Each person's body is different, however we will remind you that as your body is a physical working machine, it needs a physical power/energy force while it is preparing to be all light. As it moves further into the Ascension process, its needs will change again; it may then require less food. Listen to your body. Recognise the foods that feed your body energy, and those that deplete and tire your body. Feed it what it needs rather than what you believe it requires.

To summarise, Ascension is the process whereby the physical body and aspects contained within are systematically transcended from a low vibratory rate (third dimension) to a high vibratory rate (fifth dimension). The incarnate moves out of the energy of fear, pain and suffering which resonates with the third dimension and into love, harmony, acceptance and unity that are sustainable in the fifth dimension. The physical, emotional, mental and energetic bodies of the incarnate will go through an intensive 'clearing out' as the body as a whole sheds the old vibrations and energies to make way for the new. What begins is an intensive period of discovering debris, releasing it, accepting higher vibrations, integrating them, and then releasing more debris and so on. This cycle can go on for many years with some believing it never ends! The beauty of the cycle is that each round brings the incarnate deeper insight, happiness, consolidation and wisdom. People generally find that the cycles become more comfortable the further up the spiral they travel.

CHAPTER ELEVEN

Ascension and Life Changes

ST GERMAIN WITH LORD JERUSALEM AND LADY JERUSALEM:

I, St Germain, I, Lord Jerusalem and I, Lady Jerusalem will now come forth and dedicate a chapter to talking about Ascension and the many changes it brings. We have previously discussed Ascension and briefly touched on some of the changes. We shall now discuss in detail the various stages of Ascension and their impact on the initiate's life.

Ascension is an upward movement through the frequencies into a higher level of awareness. This leap from relative unawareness to complete awareness obviously doesn't happen overnight, and in instances where it does, it may still take the initiate many years to integrate the experience. Just as the leap in consciousness takes many years, so do the life changes of the initiate. From the very moment an initiate chooses to Ascend (usually unconscious at this stage), his life will begin to change in order to accommodate this choice. These life changes come about not only as a way of assisting the initiate to Ascend, but to live in a way that reflects ascended consciousness.

Ascension and Social Groups

As an initiate moves further up within the frequencies, his social interactions may shift and change. The initiate may require times of intense social interaction, as this level of connection with others creates a platform to integrate spiritual shifts. People benefit from spending time together as they have the opportunity to reflect on their interactive abilities by observing their own social behaviour. Social interaction can greatly assist in the Ascension process as it can draw the initiate out of himself and into the world. Once he is out of himself, he can turn around and look at himself from a different perspective.

There will be times however that isolation or a relatively low level of interaction is required. The initiate may seek to enter into himself and desire no outside stimulation or feedback. He may feel drawn to deep levels of meditation, drawing/artwork or other creative pursuits, writing, contemplation and resting. These periods can be soul-restoring and healing and have great advantages in supporting spiritual development. Others may find it beneficial to live in a reclusive and creative way with a like-minded partner or close friend. In this way, similar levels of spiritual development can be achieved, as the initiate is required to interact in a developing committed and focused way. Distraction is minimal and thus both parties come to face themselves through looking in the mirror; the mirror being the other party. This process has many rewards in the sense that it assists in developing compassion, tolerance, commitment and highly tuned communication skills.

Ascension and Preference

As Ascension raises the initiate to new heights, so does it raise his awareness of life and appreciation for certain things. What might have been attractive pre-awakening, will begin to shift slightly in the beginning of Ascension and alter dramatically as the initiate progresses along the upward path. As the initiate Ascends, he becomes more finely tuned to energy of a higher or lower vibration. As you would expect, the higher the initiate travels in himself, the less attractive lower vibrations seem. This is not to say that lower vibrations are less divine than higher ones. It is to say that the initiate's preference will alter depending on his vibration at the time. As the initiate continues to Ascend his preferences will refine.

You may find personally that your preference in people, music, literature, television programs, conversation and hobbies have altered significantly since you began consciously committing to your spiritual path. Even though age and maturity are contributing factors to preference change, you are drawn to certain areas more so than others because of your Ascension process. Your tolerance of lower vibrations will also alter. You will be less likely to expose yourself to bouts of negativity from people, films or literature. You become more discerning as you tune in to what raises your energy levels and what pulls them down. You become more genuine in yourself and so seek only things that mirror this.

Due to your changing preferences, you remove disruptive elements from your life. Disruptive elements may be diversions – things that divert your attention from your highest path, or painful relationships or behaviours that bring suffering into your home. These developing levels of discernment allow you to make responsible choices for yourself and possibly your family. We are not here to make judgements for you on what preferences are 'Ascension-like' and which ones are not. We are here to explain that your life will change as a result of Ascension, and your refining preferences will contribute to new levels of harmony achieved in your life. These changes in your preferences harmonise and balance you, and reflect your shift in awareness.

Ascension and Time

Ascension moves the initiate into higher levels of performance and competency at each new stage and phase. Just when he thought he couldn't be more organised, responsible and efficient, Ascension will challenge him further to become all that he truly can be. Over the initiate's journey he will come to be 100 per cent aware of how he uses time in his day. At each moment the initiate will become consciously aware of every choice he has. While he is learning to utilise this new found awareness, the initiate may feel disappointed with himself as he comes to realise how much time is wasted with thoughts of anger, blame and self-sabotage. As the initiate works with the energy of this ability, he will come to consciously catch himself in the moment of negativity and say:

"Ah ha, now I choose differently."

If however he still chooses to be angry, we do not judge this. He is consciously choosing to be angry and is taking full conscious responsibility for the choice.

"Ah ha, I've caught myself in a moment of anger. I choose to allow

my anger, to feel it and to ride it right through. I embrace my choice and take responsibility for it."

We are sure you can appreciate how liberating these two scenarios are. Pre-ascension, there was little accountability for time spent in ways that were not upwardly moving, nor was there an awareness of how things could be done differently. Humanity is now empowered with these new shifts in understanding about time and how it directly relates to creativity and the individual.

Let's say for example that an initiate wakes up in the morning with 100 per cent energy available to him. Five per cent of that energy is consumed with early morning thoughts about difficulties with the boss. Five per cent is spent worrying about there being no fresh clothes because when he could have been washing (last night) he was watching television to avoid thinking about work and his boss. A further ten per cent is consumed with overall worries about finances and the money that is required to fund all his complicated needs and wants. Then finally, another five per cent of energy is used worrying about the woman who has recently left him because he is not, 'emotionally or mentally available'.

Aside from each point of energy wastage creating the next energy wastage in this vicious cycle, the total 25 per cent of energy wasted per day could quite possibly go towards creating something wonderful instead of setting up a pattern of self-defeating behaviour in this man's life.

Ascension gives each initiate the ability to inquire into his own energy wastage in the moment the initiate catches himself doing it. As he awakens more deeply, Ascension and time begin to work together until Ascension transforms his understanding of time completely.

Ascension and Responsibility

As the initiate Ascends, a new understanding emerges in regard to responsibility in all areas of life. The meaning of responsibility to the initiate, adjusts to reflect the upward moving process of Ascension. Any tendencies the initiate may have towards over-responsibility or irresponsibility will be made apparent to him as the personal development process of Ascension unfolds naturally. He will more closely examine belief systems that he has inherited from family or society as he embarks upon the journey of clearing out limitations.

If he believed that it was his role to take responsibility for everyone else's happiness in his family because that's what his mother did, he may look at this and decide that it is a belief system that he no longer needs. If he watched his father throw his emotions around and blame everybody for his unhappiness, he may find he has similar tendencies of taking little responsibility for his emotional state, or may have attracted someone into his life that is like his father.

In observing his own patterns and that of his family's, the area of responsibility which is so important in Ascension will be resolved and understood. When appropriate levels of responsibility are taken, the initiate is liberated. He becomes empowered through the embracing of his own power, manifested in the physical world as responsibility. He becomes his own Master and is empowered by his own self-respect.

Ascension and Love

Ascension brings a higher love into the initiate's life. A higher love may manifest in the form of deeper connectedness with siblings, children, parents, friends, husband, wife or partner. The initiate will feel moments of heart-bursting love and joy and initially this may surprise, frighten or bring conflicting emotions up to the surface.

As he/she continually develops this openness, his heart feels safer to open and expand even further. His heart's influence in his life will be demonstrated by the new level of care, appreciation, and dedication the initiate has for areas of his life. Things that he used to be passionate about years ago will come up again to be explored. His heart will desire to express itself through creative pursuits such as cooking, art, sewing, sculpture, music, dance, writing and or acts of kindness towards others. Nature, if it doesn't already, will play a strong part in his life. The initiate will rejoice more deeply in the miraculous occasions in nature. He will become more sensitive to the shifts and changes of the Earth and will take more mindful care of animals, plants and trees.

The love that intensifies in him will show itself in the way he cares for himself, his home, work and loved ones. The initiate's gratitude shall increase manifesting even more love and abundance in his life. He explores any areas of his life that contain fear and transforms them into light. This does not mean that he will have to dig through every aspect of his psyche to draw out the fear, but it will mean that situations in life will present to aid him in transcending fear. What will be important is that he uses the situations that present as opportunities to clear limitations and fear.

CHAPTER TWELVE

Aspect Therapy

Healing as Ascension

Lord Lemuria and St Germain:

I, Lord Lemuria and I, St Germain will now come forth and speak of the healing side of Ascension. As humans Ascend, they embark upon a process of not only gaining greater insight and awareness but healing what they have become over time. Over years of pain and suffering, a human builds walls of stone and fortresses of protection to hold his inner, sensitive aspects in safety. It is the aspects that are the 'guards' of these sensitive aspects that are the damaged ones in need of nurturing, love and support to gently guide them back to their true nature. It is these 'guard' aspects that manifest themselves as the defensive, protective self, the survivor self, the manipulative self, the victim self and the aggressive self.

Originally, an aspect was like a shard of Light from the main source of Light. The main source of Light is the Soul; the shards extending out from this are the aspects. A Soul, in order to experience itself, created a Hierarchy structure so that it can have many aspects of itself living in many levels and dimensions of experience, simultaneously.

Each individual aspect contains within it, the signature frequency (the essence) of the Soul, the Soul memory and the connective frequency of the Soul so that it may reconnect to and always be connected to, all other aspects of itself. It may also have particular programming that was decided upon by the Higher Council of Higher Self, depending on what its assignments are. This programming comes from the Star Core Command.

All aspects are unique and have characteristics that individualise them from other aspects, however they are still part of the Soul. The personalities of aspects create the diversity of a Hierarchy. Diversity brings experience, expansion, creative potential, knowledge, wisdom and opportunities for learning to a Hierarchy and is thus nurtured and encouraged by councils. An aspect always has a unique and relevant task in the Hierarchy. Its tasks are its core contribution and responsibility within the structure. For example some aspects may be the musical aspects, the sexual aspects, the practical aspects, the mothering/fathering aspects etc. Because each and every Hierarchy is 100 per cent self-sufficient, it has all aspects with all abilities required for perfect creation contained within it.

The healing of aspects is necessary if these aspects have adopted skills and training from external influences in order to best guard their sensitive aspects. These aspects can be defensive, manipulative, and enraged etc, depending on their experience. Originally these aspects were loving – they have simply covered over their essential nature. It is the will to survive and to protect himself from the harshness of the exterior world that forces a human to adopt characteristics that are not true to his real Core Self.

Because Ascension is about living in the Light – not surviving in harshness, as the initiate begins to Ascend, the survival instinct and its various characteristics come to the surface. As the initiate feels supported in the Ascension process, the need to be tough and strong in an aggressive sense diminishes. As he connects to aspects of his Inner Self, his Hierarchy and his Spiritual Family, fear and issues of loneliness, abandonment and isolation lose their power. The initiate feels divinely loved, appreciated and connected and although initially these feelings may not be overly strong, he has an inner knowing that they will strengthen. It is in this way that the healing and Ascension process of an individual becomes one and the same. **An individual cannot Ascend into a new level of awareness until he is healed enough to live in that level.** Ascension itself automatically takes him through all stages of healing as a function of its process.

Every person on the personal healing path is also on the Ascension path. Even if the only desire of the person on the healing path is to feel better about himself and live a happier life, having no understanding of Ascension nor conscious intention to Ascend, he shall still Ascend. This is the nature of healing; it automatically moves and restores an aspect in that set of frequencies and elevates the person to the next frequency band of evolution.

As in Ascension, a person on the personal healing path may reach a level of healing and choose to heal no further. This simply means that the individual will stay in the dimensional and frequency experience that he is in, gaining further knowledge and wisdom and expanding himself in that level until he is ready to move onwards again. No matter what the choice is, a being cannot stop learning and growing, for each and every experience brings expansion and growth.

So how do you heal the limiting, fearful aspects? First it is important to recognise the aspects that have strayed from their original state of love. Take note of those thoughts, feelings and behaviours that do not seem to benefit you in life, leaving you with a sinking or uncomfortable feeling. Look at patterns that recur, negatively impacting on the positive potential of situations.

Gather the evidence by watching and observing these patterns and behaviours and by using the evidence, try to identify the aspect. Is the aspect part of your child self? What age? What happened to that child self that may have fractured the wholeness of the aspect, and removed it from its true core being into thoughts, feelings and behaviours that do not serve you?

This exploration can be done in the 'Aspect Therapy Meditation'. Practice this meditation often to systematically heal aspects of yourself and thus restore yourself to love.

Aspect Therapy Meditation

- Gently close your eyes, relax your body and breathe deeply and calmly.
- Allow your mind to take you to a safe place. This may be a place from your past, a current place or a place that your mind creates.
- In this safe place sense that there is a higher presence with you. Allow this Being of Light to come and rest beside you as you sit comfortably.
- This Being of Light is here to support you and hold the light for you.
- Call forth an aspect of you that would like healing now.

- As the aspect nears you take note of what it feels and looks like. You may or may not receive a lot of visual information. Use the information you have, to connect with the aspect to understand why it has come today.

- Communicate with the aspect by asking it why it has come. What would it like you to know and understand in order to be healed today?

- Ask it to open up about its true inner feelings, its pain, its fears, its anger.

- When you feel it has finished communicating, ask it to accompany the Being of Light that is with you to a cylinder of light.

- The cylinder of light shall appear in the corner of your safe place. The cylinder is designed to transport the aspect of you seeking healing into the heavens. Once in these Higher Realms, the Angelic Beings will escort the aspect of you to a place of healing.

- As the aspect of you is transported up into the heavens, focus on the cylinder of light until it disappears from your view.

- Thank the Being of Light for assisting you. You may even stay with the being for extra healing.

- When you are ready, return from your safe place and back to your body. Gently open your eyes.

CHAPTER THIRTEEN

Past Life Resolution and Aspect Therapy

ST GERMAIN AND LADY MAITREYA:

I, St Germain will now speak to thee of past lives and their purpose in a Soul's journey. To begin with, look at a Soul's journey as a time line. The beginning of the time line does not start in this life. It started many centuries ago, and it may not have started on Earth. Each Soul has a plan that drives the direction of the time line. The plan determines which point in the time line the Soul sends an aspect down to Earth to incarnate. The Hierarchy will work with the Soul, the higher levels of itself, to determine the best possible use of the time line to fulfil the objective of the plan. An objective may be to incarnate 'X' amount of aspects to evolve and expand the Hierarchy 10,000 fold, and assist in the evolution of Earth whilst contributing to the healing of fellow spiritual brothers and sisters. Compared to the mission statements of some Hierarchies, this is a very general objective as they can be very in-depth and detailed.

A Soul may utilise many centuries in order to manifest its plan and will use the gift of time and all resources required within its Hierarchy and Spiritual Family to fulfil its objective. The ability to incarnate on a time line such as Earth's time/space matrix is a gift to many Hierarchies and Souls. An aspect can incarnate as a human in the 13th Century and anchor information physically and energetically that he can return to retrieve in the 20th Century. In his 13th Century life he may have understood things that couldn't be expressed in society at the time or he may have tapped into parts of his own spirituality that he could not manifest creatively in that life. When he returns in the 20th Century he can utilise meditation to tap back into that wisdom and combined with the technology now available, manifest it physically into his world. His Higher Council can use history books, the writings, stories, poetry and artwork of others to trigger his memory banks to want to retrieve his 13th Century life. The Incarnation Council has a role in this area of development and memory. It is part of their task to put enough things in front of the incarnate to trigger his memory banks so that he remembers who he is and what he is doing or supposed to be doing upon Earth's floor.

One could ask, 'If the individual was going to retrieve the information in the 20th Century anyhow, what is the point of first incarnating in the 13th Century?'

I would say to that, that it is a good question! There is however, a logical explanation. Sometimes there is a depth and maturity required by the incarnate before he can properly utilise the information and the power of the wisdom that he holds. By incarnating into a time where he holds such wisdom and power but cannot introduce it to the world, he is required to sit back and wait. In doing so he is given the opportunity (possibly over a number of lifetimes) to understand the power of what he actually holds, rather than see it as a part of himself which he takes for granted. The incarnate also builds up motivating levels of desire to see the wisdom or gift shared with others as he experiences the frustration of not being able to share his gifts and hence a part of himself at all.

As a result of being in a human body he also has the opportunity to experience pain whether it be physical, mental or emotional. His desire to alleviate such suffering for himself and to see the end of suffering for others strengthens so deeply that it becomes a passion. That passion in some can be a force to be reckoned with and can lead individuals to choose incarnation assignments of the highest degree of difficulty but so rich in reward for many. I can think of many through history, and now more than ever, who have chosen to rise above limiting circumstances and become extraordinary in their own self healing and development and as an example to many.

A Hierarchy will often incarnate an aspect lifetime after lifetime to educate him about who he is in order to have him share such greatness with humanity. This can be challenging to explain so I like to use an analogy.

Imagine the colour white. White has always been white. It doesn't really even know it's white and to tell you the truth, it has never really thought about it. It has been happy just being white. It is then told that people need to know about white, they need some white in their lives and White needs to go and teach others about how to achieve this. White has absolutely no idea about white, it just Is! "I am White, I just Am", White says.

White incarnates in many different forms and wears different cloaks. Sometimes he wears the colour blue or green to get another perspective, but underneath the cloak he is still white. White experiences himself in the illusion of not being white and even observes others that seem to be white to understand what white is. He talks to others about himself and about themselves to learn more and more. Eventually White feels that he knows himself, he incarnates again as his true self and begins expressing or teaching his gift, his essence to the world for the purpose of his own development and the healing and expansion of others.

It is important not to judge the past incarnations that you may discover, for you may have been like White, experiencing what you are not in order to know who you really are. You, like White, may be discarding all of the cloaks that you have worn in past lives and in this one, so that you can know your true essence again in the experience as well as in the observation of it. Past lives are not to be judged for they also have another gift, the ability to recognise that regardless of how far you believe you have strayed from your true essence, it is just like in the case of White; remember to take off the cloak of different colours and what you truly are, remains eternally alive underneath.

Lady Maitreya will now take you on a journey to heal any past lives or remove any cloaks that may be blocking you from remembering and experiencing the true divine essence that you are.

I, Lady Maitreya will now come forth and speak of the relevance of Aspect Therapy in past life resolution and clearing. Past life experiences are not always essential to know in detail for often they are resolved and complete in the life they were experienced and that chapter of the Soul's journey is closed. There are other cases where the past life still bleeds like a gaping wound or a person's cloak of illusion is so tightly worn that it squashes his ability to see his own light. There is healing that can be done for this and yet it has been the way that individuals have not associated present life pain with past life experiences.

To give an example, the individual knows that something isn't quite right either through self-defeating patterns that continually arise or through unexplained fears that are always underlying. It is here that the individual may develop the desire to find out the truth and set himself free. In many cases, patterns and fears are developed in childhood. He may explore his childhood deeply and find the answers to many of his questions about his own behaviours. In situations where there doesn't seem to be any resolution on certain patterns or fears, it is helpful to scratch the surface of time and travel back into previous incarnations. The individual may find the answers to deep and pressing questions that have plagued him for years by connecting to an aspect of himself that lived centuries ago.

As St Germain has previously discussed, past life travel is beneficial, not only to heal such gaping wounds but to call forth skills, knowledge and wisdom from previous incarnations and use them in the present.

There are a number of ways to connect with either your ancient wisdom or the aspects of you that want healing. I, Lady Maitreya will now explain one way which can be exceptionally powerful.

Instead of using straight Aspect Therapy, we put forward a different intention where we use the stage of the Great Hall and invite your past life aspects to join us. The Great White Hall exists in the fifth dimension and is a meeting place for many Beings of Light. In the Great White Hall your aspects can communicate with you and share their story. They may wish to be healed and in which case, they can utilise the cylinder of violet or white light. If they wish to pass on their wisdom, they may talk for some time or simply sit with you passing on healing and wisdom vibrationally and telepathically. After you return from meditation, you may find it beneficial to write down the information you received.

Below is the Past Life Aspect Therapy Meditation, you may wish to record the meditation on tape and play it back to yourself.

Past Life Aspect Therapy Meditation

- Visualise your spirit slowly lifting up and out of your body. From its new viewpoint, your spirit can see the whole room that your body is lying in.
- Your spirit floats up to the ceiling, through the roof, and to a height where you can see the rooftops of any local buildings.
- Moving higher up now, you begin to see not only your area, but also neighbouring suburbs or surrounding countryside.
- As you float higher and higher, you begin to feel as though you are moving out of the Earth's atmosphere.
- You can see Earth below as you move further out into the galaxy.
- You can feel the velvety blackness of the galaxy all around you.
- Up ahead you can see the shimmering lights of distant stars and worlds, however we are not going there today, we are going somewhere else...
- In the blackness of the galaxy, you can see not far from you, an outline of a door.
- You can tell it is a door against the blackness of the galaxy as the light from the realm on the other side of the door shines through it.
- Float over to the door and place your hand on the door handle.
- Gently open the door and step onto the lush green lawn of the realm you are now connecting to.
- Shut the door behind you and walk across the lawn.
- Above you, you can feel the blueness of the sky, the warm sunshine on your face and ahead of you, the gentle spray of mist from the water features that grace the garden.
- As you look ahead, beyond the water features, you see the magnificent and massive, 'Great White Hall'. From the hall extends a fan of white marble steps.
- Allow yourself to walk towards the Great White Hall, drinking in its beauty and strength.

- As you walk closer to the hall, you notice that its two massive entrance doors are opening slightly.
- A beautiful Being of Light steps out and stands on the marble steps.
- This being is to be your guide and support in all that we are about to do.
- Sit down with this Being of Light on a sun couch positioned at the top of the marble steps.
- From this new position you can feel the sunshine on your face and see over the whole garden.
- Connect with the Being of Light that is with you. Feel safe with this energy of divinity by feeling its love and support for you.
- Put your intention forward that you would now like to resolve any past life aspect or situations that will serve your highest good for these moments in time.
- In the distance you can sense that there is a part of you desiring to reconnect with you. It may be a higher aspect, or it may be in pain, it is not yet clear. What is clear is that it is a part of you from a different time.
- As this aspect nears you begin to sense certain characteristics it has. You may sense its age, gender and possibly cultural distinctions. Study the aspect of you to gather as much information as possible.
- The aspect now stands in front of you. Ask the aspect why has it come. What would it like to tell you in order to set itself free? Communicate openly with the aspect in order to understand the whole story. The aspect may show you visions of where it has come from as a way of explaining itself. If your aspect shows you a scene of its past life experience, stay with it for as long as it takes to understand the issue and then invite the aspect back to the Great Hall for healing.
- When you have finished communicating, invite the aspect to be guided by the Being of Light beside you into a cylinder of white light. This cylinder waits patiently to take the aspect up into the heavens for healing. The aspect has been released to the Higher Realms when you can no longer see the cylinder.

- Allow yourself to thank the Being of Light and start to make your way back across the lawn to the door that you came in through.
- At the door ask the Being of Light if it is staying here in the vicinity of the Great Hall, or is it returning to Earth with you.
- Either way, bring the love of this Being of Light with you as you step into the galaxy and shut the door behind you.
- Feel yourself floating down through the galaxy and closer into the earth's atmosphere. Move towards the building where your body lies.
- Connect once again with your body and ground completely into it.
- Gently move your hands and toes and reconnect with Earth's floor again.
- Take a deep breath and when you are ready slowly open your eyes.

Record any insights you have received in your journal.

CHAPTER FOURTEEN

The Earth and Sea Realms

The Support of The Earth

LORD AND LADY NEPTUNE:

There is no coincidence in humanity Ascending on and in conjunction with Mother Earth. Every single tool an initiate could possibly need is on Earth. Every mystery within every realm of this galaxy has its replica on Earth. For Earth in truth is a storehouse, a library, and an encyclopaedia. Just as a set of encyclopaedias record and display the many facets of this world, so is Earth the encyclopaedia for the galaxy.

As you begin to connect into Earth, its treasures are revealed to you. It is here in this journey of initiation that the mysteries of the planet are released into your psyche. What was formally unknown to you becomes known and experienced. It is one thing to be told the mysteries by another and a totally different thing to know them and experience their power.

Use this power of the Earth and her realms to support and accelerate your spiritual awakening and to teach and train you on your unique path.

The Triad of the Earth, the Seas and the Nature Realms

We, Lord and Lady Neptune speak of the strength of the seas, the Earth and the Nature Realms. These three energies are bound together in love and in a force of light that acts as a powerful triad of energies for all those on Earth wishing to Ascend. The initiate's Ascension process is accelerated as he/she connects to this triad. The triad acts as a vehicle to transport the initiate upwardly to connect to the Higher Realms, and downwardly into the Earth, the grounding foundation from which the initiate receives support.

The initiate sits *inside* this triad of energies and draws from the various strengths of each realm.

The Sea Realms

The Oceanic Realms of Earth have immense power and ability to aid in the Ascension of humanity. The Earth's sea is made up of many different realms. There are Angelic and Celestial Realms of the sea containing many kingdoms and families of love and light. The sea is as diverse as your world today. You are aware of the sea creatures that you can see with the human eye. There are, however, many other beings and creatures of light that can only be seen with the spiritual eye. In the Sea Realms, there are many orders and councils consisting of various Beings of Light. There are orders of the sea mothers, sea fathers, Councils of the Angelic Realms such as sea angels, and beings of a celestial frequency that bridge Earth to many other areas within the galaxy.

Although the Earth's oceans are home to many Beings of Light, they also act as doorways. These gateways open Earth up to receive information and energy from other realms within the galaxy. The oceans of Earth act as transmitters for the higher frequencies. As humanity awakens, Earth receives higher frequencies and information from the Spiritual Family of Light in various other realms. These realms use the receptiveness of the sea to pass messages to Earth vibrationally. There are many human channels on Earth's floor that have been receiving messages this way for years.

The sea also directly affects the consciousness of humanity. The sea contains higher thought forms within its structure. Humanity is drawn to the water as a way of connecting to higher levels of consciousness and leaving polluted thoughts behind. The sea acts as a cleanser of the old as well as a connector to the new. As humans learn to utilise the powerful force that is the ocean and seas of Earth, their spiritual journey will become easier and they will move through blockages, fears and limitation quicker than what they could believe. The sea is a healer within all aspects and thus aids the initiate to Ascend through healing, cleansing and reconnection.

To best utilise the kingdoms of the sea in your spiritual evolution allow yourself to sit quietly and journal-write, channel, pray and meditate by the sea as often as you can. Spend time bringing the essence of the ocean into your heart in meditation. For the swimmers, divers and surfers, the sea naturally heals you while rebuilding and cleansing the energy fields around you. You can use meditation to explore the Oceanic Realms. You meditations will introduce you to the many Beings of Light that make up the Sea Family. Please see the meditation example at the end of this chapter.

The Oceanic Realms and Healing

Archangel Couriel:

Dear Ones, I, Archangel Couriel will now speak of the Oceanic Family of Light. I am indeed an Archangel of Celestial Oceanic frequencies. I live within the realms of Earth's sea, however I travel to many other Oceanic Realms within this galaxy. My Family of Light consists of many extraordinary beings, each holding the energy for many different realms, councils, and boards of light where higher choices and decisions are made. These decisions manifest as changes occurring in the waters of Earth as well as on other oceanic worlds. Decisions may include allowing new groups of spiritual beings to spend time in the Earth's seas to gather experience or allow new levels of higher consciousness to be anchored into the waters, thus reaching and raising the consciousness and psyche of humanity.

Groups of Light Beings from various areas of the galaxy have come to the waters of Earth over many years to simply experience the wonder of water in this form. The Earth sea is unique in many ways and is a drawcard for Beings of Light as it can be experienced either in human or etheric form. Many Beings of Light enjoy the Earth's sea as it allows them to experience humanity's consciousness and collective psyche without having to incarnate as human beings.

Some Ascended Masters and Angelic Beings take on the form of a fish or sea creature as this allows the body of the creature to transmit higher frequencies to humanity. The body of a whale for example is a very powerful tool as it can accept higher frequencies being pulsed into it by Beings of Light from higher dimensions. After it accepts these higher frequencies, it can then pulse these vibrations to humanity through the waters and directly into the mental field of humanity's psyche and consciousness. Those that swim with dolphins and other sea creatures can speak of the powerfully transforming experience these creatures of light can bring. By being with these sea creatures it is easy to see why many people consider them the true healers. Just spending time either in or beside water has profound healing affects.

Many people choose to keep fish in their homes either unconsciously or consciously for the same reasons. Goldfish are able to transmit higher frequencies that oversee the healing and transformation of humanity. The fish and creatures of the lakes and rivers are to be respected for the healers they are as they hold keys to the next phase of spiritual evolution for humanity.

Meditating near your fish tank will aid you to move through blockages and Ascend through using the frequencies transmitted to you. Looking after your fish in a supportive and clear environment is of the utmost importance. Fish have the ability to work at very high levels, transmitting higher and finer frequencies constantly, providing they are in an environment compatible to their vibration. Fish are powerful healers as they bring calmness to humanity.

The use of clear quartz, amethyst, or aquamarine coloured crystals as well as healthy plant life in the water is of a profound advantage and aids the fish in their work. Some vibrations near their tank assist greatly such as the Tibetan sounds and AUM chants in a tape and CD.

Call on I, Archangel Couriel any time you choose and I will walk with you as you consciously use the power of the oceans and seas and their creatures in your healing and Ascension process. As you call upon me, you grant me permission to aid you in all the areas I specialise. I send my love to you and remind you that the Oceanic Family of Light are always around you.

Meditation for Connecting to the Earth and Oceanic Realms

- Close your eyes gently, relax your body and listen to the sounds outside the room.

- The sounds will now fade and you will feel your spirit lifting out of your body and up into the room.
- Your spirit will now lift over the building.
- It will travel as far as it needs to until it finds a clear area of Earth in the centre of the land of Australia. You will come to the desert and no-one is to be seen.
- Your spirit touches down here and you can feel the strong clear earth beneath your feet.
- You sense that you are not alone and look up to feel and possibly see an ancient guide of great power and wisdom, standing at what appears to be a cave like entrance into a large rock surrounded by many smaller rocks.
- Walk slowly over to the ancient guide. Spend time connecting with him. When he feels it is appropriate, he will grant you permission to enter the sacred place.
- After receiving his permission, allow him to guide you into the cave.
- As you enter into the cave you feel the warmth on your skin radiated by the heated rock.
- You begin to follow the path down into the cave.
- Further and further into the cave you travel.
- The path into the cave dips deeper and deeper into the Earth and begins to spiral down.
- The path becomes very steep. You reach out and touch the rocky wall of cave to support you as you descend into the Earth.
- Your guide leads you into a room-like area of the cave. You can sense that you are very deep into the Earth.
- As you step into the room-like area, you sense that you and your guide have company.
- You look around the room and see that there is an Ancient Being waiting patiently.

- He walks up to you and studies you.
- He then turns around and beckons you to follow him.
- He takes you to a strange plasma wall in the cave and tells you to prepare to step through. He explains that you will step through into a very deep part of the ocean and even though you may not be able to see, someone will take your hand and be your guide. The moment this person holds your hand, you will be able to breathe underwater and your body temperature will alter to keep you warm.
- You say goodbye and thank you to your guides.
- You step through the plasma wall and into the sea.
- Everything is very dark. You feel a soft hand reaching out to take yours and you feel instantly assured. This being is Lady Neptune.
- She guides you through the water to a rocky ledge where you both rest. Peer over the ledge to see an oceanic kingdom below.
- The kingdom is lit by a white orb of light like an ethereal moon.
- Lady Neptune leads you into the kingdom where you touch down onto a path in the middle of the oceanic city. You follow this path to a great temple.
- The steps of the temple lead you to large entrance doors. Inside this holy house a Council of Light Beings sit in a circle on the floor.
- There is a space kept for you and Lady Neptune in the circle and you both sit down.
- The council greet you and explain to you that there is an aspect of yourself they want you to meet. This is your 'oceanic self' – the oceanic representative for your Hierarchy.
- You look over towards a different entrance into the hall and see that a large Being of Light has entered the room. You stand up from the council and walk towards this magnificent being. You study this being until you are ready to embrace it, merge with it and become one with it as an aspect of you.

- Spend as much time in the Temple of Light communicating to the council and asking questions of them or Lady Neptune.

- When you are ready to leave, Lady Neptune escorts you to an area of the temple where a cylinder of light awaits to transport you to the surface.

- You thank the Council of Light and step into the cylinder. The cylinder pulls away slowly from the kingdom and moves through the sea until you see the first glimpses of sunlight touching the water.

- At the surface you see that you have been taken to the surface not far from the shore. It is here that Lady Neptune embraces you and you thank her. As she disappears back into the waters you know that you are safe to glide back to shore and the sanctuary of your home.

Earth

LORD PAN:

The Earth itself, its soil, its strength, its rock, its crystal, and its minerals are the grounding foundation the higher dimensions use in order to establish the higher frequency upon Earth's floor. The higher dimensions do use humans, oceanic creatures and animals to anchor the higher frequencies, but even these mediums must then anchor the frequencies into the Earth. The Earth stabilises these higher frequencies thus giving them the opportunity to manifest into physical form if they choose. For example the higher frequencies may ground into Earth and later its physical manifestation may be as a piece of music, a literary work, or a painting. The frequency is grounded and is connected to the person or group of people it resonates to in order to be brought into physical manifestation.

Without the Earth, the frequency would not be grounded or stabilised enough in order to be brought into a physical form. Instead it would remain a frequency of potential floating around in the ethers, unrealised and not manifested in the physical world.

In order for an individual to be all that he can be, it is essential that the grounding process is taken seriously otherwise the same rule as above applies. The Higher Self can send higher frequencies to the initiate, but if the frequencies are not anchored into the Earth, they float around in the ethers unrealised. The initiate could see the possibility of manifesting all these wonderful creative experiences, yet always feels as though they are just out of reach.

Grounding properly into the Earth eliminates such issues from occurring. People choose to ground in different ways. I, Lord Pan will list some suggestions of grounding exercises which may be integrated into your life:

1. Meditation, writing, prayer, exercise, reading, or creating art in places of natural surroundings. Such places include forests, woodlands, gardens, parks, lakes, seaside or snow.
2. Cooking, housework and gardening. Many spiritual orders over the centuries have often kept their initiates engaged in certain mundane activities as there is real power to be found in such tasks. Aside from the grounding effects, these activities clear the head, shift melancholy, encourage motivation and bring a sense of achievement to an individual.
3. Meditation, where you visualise your energy anchored to the deepest point in the Earth. Call on I, Lord Pan whilst in meditation and I will come and work with you to ensure your energies are being grounded completely.

You will begin, as a natural consequence of connecting to the Earth and Sea Realms, to gravitate to the nature kingdoms of plants and trees. Gardens and ancient trees will hold so much more significance for you. If you haven't already, you will begin to sense or even see the elemental kingdoms at work and play. Their light will shine and sparkle and you may see this from the corner of your eye. You may be drawn to learning about herbs, planting a garden and trees or having house plants. These interests will strengthen as the Nature Realms and spirits sense you are awakening and thus move closer to you.

CHAPTER FIFTEEN

The Spiritual Family

Meeting the Family

DJWHAL KHUL:

Many centuries ago a small group of energies perceived a need to support and assist humanity through its childhood, its adolescence and then into its adulthood. This small group of energies, in human terms would be considered very large, but to us it is quite a small gathering. This gathering of light is made up of higher beings all closely related in spirit and interest with a keen desire to be all that they are meant to be. They are here to evolve aspects of themselves that are incarnated on Earth whilst assisting the aspects of fellow brothers and sisters. This group is an arm of the Spiritual Hierarchy for Earth. I, Djwhal Khul am a member of this group of light.

All members of the Spiritual Hierarchy of Earth have their specialised roles, as well as contributing to roles shared by all. In this chapter we will explore a number of these roles, including the Messenger of Light, the Divine Overseer and the Christ Consciousness Companion. Any member of the Spiritual Hierarchy for Earth can volunteer to fulfil these roles for their own incarnated aspects on Earth and their brothers and sisters that are you, on Earth's floor right now. I, Djwhal Khul will now assist to explain these roles and their relevance to your life and spiritual development.

The Messenger of Light – Your Guiding Light to Transmute Your Fears and Limitations

The Messenger of Light is a Being of Light assigned to you when you decide to make the transition from fear to love. This transition is the Ascension process or the process where an individual moves out of the constraints of third dimension (the 'home base' of fear) and into fifth dimension known to many as the Christ Consciousness or Love consciousness. The purpose of the Messenger of Light is to gently guide you through levels where fear exists and initiate you into the Higher Realms of fifth dimension and beyond. The Messenger of Light is not the same as a 'spirit guide' as its task is more specific and specialised. The Messenger of Light will guide you solely and strictly for the purposes of assisting you to recognise fears and limitations that are holding you back, and then transmute them into love and forgiveness.

Your Messenger of Light can be called on at any time you feel you need the assistance of this energy of divinity. In order to strengthen and further develop your relationship with your Messenger of Light, allow yourself to sit quietly on a regular basis, daily would be ideal, and listen to any messages and guidance your Messenger of Light has to give you. Remember that the purpose of this energy of divinity is to assist you to move through blockages so call on your Messenger to lift worries, fears and anxieties from you. Before you sleep at night, beckon your Messenger and ask that you be cleared of all that no longer serves your highest good and then allow for the healing to be done as you rest.

The Divine Overseer – This Guide Holds a Copy of Your Divine Blueprint, the Plan of Your Many Lives

The Overseer is a being or an energy that has earned as a minimum, the rank and title of Ascended Master. (An Ascended Master is one who has Ascended from the third dimension into the levels of fifth and possibly through to the seventh and beyond, whilst being in a physical incarnation, yet not specifically in human form.) An Overseer is a Master with considerable soul experience and is one who stays true to the light and to the principles of love, truth, integrity and allowing.

Each individual is assigned an Overseer who volunteers for the position, before they come to Earth. The function of an Overseer is to 'check' on you through various stages of your life journey and to ensure that all is going according to plan. The Overseer holds a copy of the blueprint of your life plan and genetic structures and will alert you if there is any interference in these plans that may block you from being all that you are meant to be. Your Overseer keeps you on the right track and doesn't allow you to divert yourself too much.

Your Overseer takes great delight in being with you through major shifts in your life including your birth, your marriage, the birth of your children and your death.

Your Divine Overseer can be accessed by you, if you desire to establish your own personal contact, through sitting quietly and asking the Overseer to enter into your space. Practise with this. Don't be disappointed if it doesn't happen the way you want it to straight away. Remember that your spiritual skills will develop the more you use them and align to them.

Christ Consciousness Companion – Teaching you in the Principles of Compassion, Forgiveness, Trust, Allowing, Integrity

A Christ Consciousness Companion is a Master who has been initiated through training with He who is the Christ, as one who has attained Christ Consciousness. The training process can be likened to an apprenticeship whereby the apprentice must demonstrate a commitment to the principles that define Christ Consciousness. Such principles include compassion, forgiveness, trust, allowing all things to be and flow as they need to, and integrity. Once a Master has been initiated, 'he/she' is then assigned to an individual who wishes to attain Christ Consciousness this lifetime, and live these principles within his day to day life.

Your companion 'lives' with you and has an active role in your physical life. Your companion observes you during the day and then teaches you when you sleep at night. You learn where you can strengthen the Christ energies and principles in your life and relationships with others. Call on your companion to assist you with challenges that require extra dedication on your behalf to stay true to the Christ principles, and your companion will give you the strength that you need.

Your Christ Consciousness Companion also works in the Sun Level of your Hierarchy and acts as a bridge between you and that vibration.

Seventh Dimensional Assistance – Celestial Beings, Heavenly Tones, Enlightened Kingdoms

The soft light of the celestial frequencies and angelic guides of the seventh dimension can be hard to resist. It is easy to see why to some, this dimension is truly experienced as 'Seventh Heaven'. It is possible to live in the fifth dimension in terms of vibration and perception, and then access the seventh dimension through dreams and meditations. The celestial sounds and vibrant colour shows experienced in meditation are often gifts sent down by the Beings of Light of the seventh dimension.

Although there are many councils in the seventh dimension, there are four major councils that we shall discuss. These councils can be accessed easily by humanity, and many Light-Workers are already developing close relationships with the Beings of Light on these councils. The four councils are:

The Brotherhood of Light – A Higher Order of Divine Spiritual Service to Humanity

The Brotherhood of Light is a group of Ascended Masters, Archangels, High Lamas and other highly evolved beings that congregate on the seventh dimension and offer themselves to humanity in the way of guidance, healing and other spiritual services. I, Djwhal Khul, Lord Maitreya, Babaji, Kuthumi and various other Masters connect together to make up the Brotherhood. The Ancient Elders of the Native American, Australian Aboriginal, Tibetan and Mongolian peoples are also members of this divine council and have loyally served humanity and the planet for many centuries. The Brotherhood positions itself over the Himalayas, in the etheric, however it is transportable and can move around to different parts of the world. It can be called on by anyone who wishes to connect with this level of assistance.

The Sacred Nuns of the Essene Order – Assistance with your Gentleness, Softness and Feminine Power

This council consists of highly evolved feminine energies such as Mother Mary and many of the female saints that are known to us on Earth, including St Catherine and St Genevieve. On leaving their physical bodies, Mother Teresa and Princess Diana returned to the order to continue their service to humanity in the etheric. Lady Maitreya, Lady Chiron, Lady Sananda, Lady Kuthumi, Lady Rinpoche and many other feminine energies also assist humanity through this porthole into Earth's atmospheres and realms.

Anyone who desires nurturing, acceptance, kindness and love can pray to this council and they will hear you instantly. If you are having problems with your feminine energy, your gentleness, softening, or taking your feminine power, call on this council. They can also assist you in matters of family, children, friendships and relationships.

MOTHER MARY:

I, Mother Mary will now speak to thee of the role of the Sacred Nuns of the Essene Order. We are on Earth for the purpose of assisting humanity but are able to move through all dimensions and aid other planetary worlds as well. We are a group of higher energies that formed when we perceived a need for our combined service. We individually were very effective in assisting humanity, but as humanity's needs grew greater as a result of the times, society and its choices, we chose to rejoin our energies in a Council of Light. We liken ourselves, for the purpose of earthly understanding, to a volunteer group of leaders on Earth that band together with an interest and desire to assist a common cause. Our cause is humanity, however at these moments in time we are involved in other planetary worlds and their healing as well.

Our work here on Earth is to assist humanity to restore the feminine principle and to choose creativity, kindness and truth as essential components of daily living. Many people on Earth have prayed for assistance in such areas and have prayed to see these shifts in humanity as a permanent adjustment. It is these people that have sounded the call for all, and indeed, all do benefit.

I, Mother Mary do truly look forward to the next fifty years on the planet of Earth for I shall see many changes that shall bring forth profound shifts in perception and behaviour in humanity. This is not to say that we that are of the Higher Realms are sitting in judgement of humanity's current perceptions, for we are not. We are however looking forward to watching these profound shifts, for we see the pots of gold at the end of the rainbow in relation to humanity's development. The rainbows and gold will be a tangible gift and humanity shall make it through to the realisation and attainment of this gift.

We that are of the Sacred Nuns look forward to being called by humans to enrich their lives in a way that shall see the embracing of the feminine principle that exists within all things.

I, Mother Mary will now complete this channelling and send my love and support to all.

The Celestial Archangel Realm – Celestial Sea Angels, Earth Angels, Home Angels, Healing Angels, Children's Angels

DJWHAL KHUL:

Although this realm and its council is mainly composed of Archangels of a Celestial frequency, it has access to all other angelic realms and orders. Some of the Archangels that sit on this council are Archangel Michael, Gabriel, Raphael, Uriel, Ariel, Jasmine, Reikiel, Angela, Jophiel, Samuel and Couriel. This council is responsible for identifying the issues facing humanity and Earth, and then asking for volunteers within the realm, for assistance. For example, if you express your problem to the council, they will address what sort of assistance you need and then will ask the relevant angelic realm for volunteers. A volunteer Angelic Being will then join the council and work with them to find the best solution for you. Whenever there is a crisis on Earth's floor, this council 'recruits' the Angelic Beings with the relevant experience and sends them to Earth.

If you wish to connect with angelic lights that can assist you to heal your problems, speak to this loving council and they can assist you. It is important to know that there is an angel or angelic energy that can help you with any problem that you may have, as the angelic realms specialise in certain areas. There are home angels, healing angels, heart angels, sea angels, earth angels, angels for guiding children, teenagers, mothers and fathers. For every issue that could ever cause pain to humanity, there is an angel dedicated to finding its cure, so call on the Angelic Council for they are more than pleased to assist you.

Stop for a moment and call forth an issue that has been troubling your mind and interrupting your peace. Ask the Angelic Beings to aid you with this issue and visualise yourself handing it over in a box to the council. Trust that the Angelic Beings will tend to your request instantly and there shall be some relief for you in a very short space in time. Practise this exercise regularly for relief from burdens and worries.

The God and Goddess Higher Council – Each and Every Person on Earth's Floor has Aspects of Themselves on this Council

The God and Goddess Higher Council is an energy band that exists within the seventh dimension. From the seventh dimension it connects through all other dimensions to be accessible to Earth and humanity. Each and every person on Earth has higher aspects of himself or herself that sit on this council.

When you personally connect to this council, you not only connect to Gods and Goddesses of other Hierarchies, but higher masculine and feminine aspects of yourself. You can call upon the Gods and Goddesses that sit on this council and they will assist you to connect to your own God and Goddess levels. The council members, Sanat Kumara, Lord and Lady Venus, Mount Olympus, Lord and Lady Neptune, Lord and Lady Gaia, Pan and his feminine balance, Lord and Lady Jerusalem, Lord Jesus and Mary Magdalene, Pallas Athena and her masculine balance, Djwhal Khul, Quan Yin and countless others are here to aid you directly.

The council also has many planetary roles in the healing and development of Earth and humanity. The council works on other planetary worlds not well known to mankind, and takes on an overseeing role as well as an active one depending on the need. Through this council the massive healing rays that manifest as towers of light are grounded. The council works closely with the Council of the Directorship of the Rays and directs and determines how rays are distributed. If, for example, there is a crisis in the Middle East, the council may increase the light ray intensity that is being sent to that part of the world.

You can call on this council to direct healing rays into your body and into your home or workplace. The more people that request the rays, the more the council can help humanity, for they are restricted in how much they can help, until you grant them permission.

Ancient Spiritual Family – Your Ancient Spiritual Family Sits Around Your Hierarchy; Nurturing, Protecting and Creating with You

Your ancient Spiritual Family is referred to as 'ancient' because they are of a lineage not always related to your current earthly family and have existed before the creation of Earth itself. Your ancient family assisted in the creation not only of the spirit that you are now, but the expansiveness that is your soul as well. Many spiritual Masters spend periods of their life of spiritual practice, dedicated to reconnecting with their ancient lineage.

As you have already discovered a Hierarchy is a geometrical design structure of light, colour and sound, in which a soul keeps all of its aspects, memory banks, abilities, gifts and so on. The physical incarnation of you on Earth right now is merely one aspect of this soul that has many millions of aspects existing simultaneously and these may not necessarily be in human form. Your Hierarchy has many functions within the All that Is that ensures the smooth running of the galaxy and the universe.

Your ancient Spiritual Family sits around your Hierarchy – nurturing you, protecting you and creating with you. Some of your spiritual brothers and sisters you may know as friends or family this lifetime, as often a Spiritual Family will incarnate within close proximity to each other. You also have spiritual parents, grandparents, Godparents and elders that assist you and the developments within your Hierarchy.

Meditation, prayer, journal writing, personal ceremonies and quiet time alone will help you to reconnect with your Spiritual Family and allow for you to tap into the infinite knowledge and wisdom that has been gained by your great lineage. Allow yourself to sit quietly, breathe and ask for them to reconnect to you and establish themselves into your heart.

Ascended Masters

"We urge you to travel into the stillness within. Feel our presence with you and our love for you that is boundless."

HIGHER COUNCIL OF ASCENDED MASTERS:

We, of the Higher Council of Ascended Masters come today to explain our tasks upon Earth's floor. We have been to Earth many times before in human bodies to lift and evolve the consciousness and psyche of humanity. We are now here, in spirit form as your guides and guardians to lead you to the realisation of your own spiritual light and divine purpose. Some of us discovered our light and purpose many centuries ago and contributed this awareness to the benefit of the world. We have come to aid you to do the same so that Earth and all upon her can reach freedom individually, and as a global family.

In order to become an Ascended Master all of us have ascended in our various lifetimes whilst holding our human bodies, into a higher state of self-understanding and awareness of the realms in which we exist. We come to offer you the benefit of our insight into your life purpose and spiritual development. As you call upon us, we can begin now to aid you to realise your higher purpose within the practical aspect of your life as well as on the inner plane. Our assistance is always at your service.

Our love for you is so deep that it cannot be fully explained; only experienced. We urge you to travel into the stillness within and feel our presence with you and our love for you that is boundless.

We thank you for taking the time to understand our purpose in your life for as you do you connect to us even more and aid us to truly aid you. As you read this book, we stand beside you sharing our love and healing vibrations with you. You are now remembering your higher purpose on Earth and the divine Spiritual Family that guides you from above. Enjoy your journey, Dear One, for it holds many blessings for you.

Building a Stronger Connection with the Masters and Spiritual Family

DJWHAL KHUL:

Ascended Masters are Beings of Light who come to Earth in spirit form to be of service to humanity. They have lived on Earth in various incarnations over the centuries, and have often made inspiring contributions to the development of humanity. They are closer to Earth than ever before to aid humanity as it shifts into greater spiritual awareness.

As with all relationships, communication is essential in creating the foundation of a long lasting and trusting union. To develop your relationship with the Masters and Spiritual Family, communicate. Talk to them about how you feel, what your fears are, and all the 'ins and outs' of your life. It is here that you learn to keep your counsel with the Masters and in time you begin to trust them to listen to all of your prayers and concerns.

There are many different ways to begin this journey of communication. You may begin by finding a safe place to rest. This safe place may be in your home or somewhere in nature. Ensure that your safe place is warm and comfortable. Sit quietly and close your eyes. Simply breathe in and out and feel the calming effect of following your breathing until your mind begins to relax and your body lets go. Now in your peaceful state call in the Beings of Light to enter into the space around you. Continue your breathing as you begin to feel heavenly energies descending into your awareness.

In time you may feel safe to allow the Beings of Light to bring their energies down into your body. As they enter into your body you may feel light, heavy, happy, emotional or a little tired. There is no right or wrong sensation or emotion that you can experience. If you do not feel a connection straight away, take time to build the bridge between you and the higher beings by repeating the exercise everyday. Be patient as the connection can take time to establish itself.

The next stage is to allow yourself to communicate your feelings whilst being in this calm and connected space. Use your time with the Masters to download all of your fears and concerns by simply talking. Ask them for assistance in all areas of your life that you are worried about and they shall come forth and aid you. Pray about your dreams and desires knowing that they shall be answered and fulfilled. Ask for the Higher Beings to not only give you what you want, but to show you how to create it for yourself. In time you will begin to sense that they are communicating back to you through situations, signs and thoughts. You may receive even deeper insights during or after your meditation.

After some time you may find that you hear words or even receive visions when you are in this quiet space. Develop this by continuing your practice and in time you will open to long conversations with the Masters and Beings of Light. Remember that they are always here for you, they are never too busy and will never abandon you. Often people feel as though what is occurring in their lives is too trivial to discuss with the Masters. This is not the case as the Higher Beings encourage communication on all levels and about all things. They understand a relationship is best built by being completely open.

Call on the Ascended Masters and Spiritual Family both in your day to day life and during your meditations. Feel your heart lighten and your life improve as you invite such divine assistance to walk beside you.

CHAPTER SIXTEEN

Guides and Guardians – Their Profiles

Author's Notes: The following pages are profiles of some of the Beings of Light that work within the Spiritual Hierarchy for Earth and have a direct role in aiding humanity. These beings can come forth and aid you in many different areas of your practical life as well as your spiritual development. Through reading the profiles you are able to understand their various roles and through this understanding, develop a relationship with these beings.

The best way to develop such a relationship as with any relationship, is to invest in communication. Speak openly to the Beings of Light working with you. Allow yourself to open up by expressing to them your worries, fears, dreams and higher goals. Read through the profiles to familiarise yourself with the tasks and personalities of these beings. Begin establishing your relationship with them for they are part of your network of assistance on the physical plane.

Djwhal Khul

I, Djwhal Khul have many functions on Earth at these moments in time. Although I serve all aspects of Earth I particularly focus on the Tibetan region of this world. My energies can be felt in Tibet and its surrounding lands as my spirit dances through its waters, homes and consciousness. I sit on many ethereal councils that base themselves within this vicinity including the Himalayan Brotherhood of Light, the Higher Council of Nepal and the Tibetan spiritual councils of the Temples.

I work often with my spiritual sister Quan Yin as we harmonise the vibrations between her spiritual home of China and mine of Tibet. We hold the energy between the two lands and create a synergy of frequencies that call many higher Masters to Earth to be of service to humanity. We can be heard singing and chanting together by those with the spiritual ear who take the time to listen to our songs of light. Many a traveller has felt our presence beside them as they venture through this part of the world.

I, Djwarl Khul work in many other ways including roles that I hold with the Ascended Master St Germain. Together we aid the Children of Earth in their plight to discover their inner light and spiritual heritage. We have a parental role on some levels and can be called upon to offer direct aid and assistance. I often work with those young Light-Workers that need confirmation in their journey, however even the older ones call upon me for advice and direction. As I am a member of the Law of One council I can be of assistance to those Light-Workers that are challenged when making decisions. I can assist them to choose that which has the highest possible outcome for all concerned. The Law of One Council ensures that harmony prevails through the universe by guiding each soul through their choices.

As keeper of the Emerald Ray, I have other roles alongside the Law of One Council. The Emerald Ray has a bridging capacity and aids initiates to remember the masculine side of their hearts. I hold the energy for those men on the spiritual path that desire to reconnect into their heart chakras but feel blocked out of fear or simply lack of knowledge and awareness. My role is to educate humanity on the role of the masculine side of the heart and how to reconnect to it. The masculine aspect of the heart houses True Love, whereas the feminine side houses Unconditional Love.

Affirmation
"I ask Djwhal Khul to be a mentor and guide for me. I thank him for his spiritual counsel and friendship."

Keywords: Tibetan Consciousness, Emerald Ray, Law of One, Choices, True Love.

Sanat Kumara

I, Sanat Kumara have a fatherly role with humanity and the welfare of each and every soul upon Earth's floor. I maintain a bridge of connection between humanity and the Ancient Beings that live within this universe. My task is to ensure the unification of the Spiritual Hierarchy for Earth and the Spiritual Family. Each and every person on Earth's floor is a member of our Spiritual Family. I remind the Family of this truth and seek to establish peace between all parties. I belong to many Sacred Councils and Boards of Light and often make choices designed to bring forth a deeper level of connectedness between those on Earth and the higher planes.

There are many beings that do not have a direct role as Ascended Masters or Angelic and Celestial Energies on Earth. As a result they do not have a close working relationship with humanity. I have chosen to enable humanity to still benefit from the wisdom and support from these other energies by being the bridge of connection. I see myself as the connection station! Through me many people on Earth receive channels to realms and beings that they otherwise may not connect to. Call upon me and I will guide you to reconnect with new Masters and other Beings of Light that are not commonly known to humanity. I can aid you to open your channels so that you too can have a direct dialogue with the Higher Realms.

I have been blessed with the opportunity to sit on a Higher Council that directs healing rays to humanity as well as my other role as a bridge. Healing rays are literally Beings of Light that are here to bring healing and inspiration to the world. On the council of the Directorship of the Rays, I work to ensure that healing reaches all areas of the world that request it. I am pleased to watch the transformation that takes place when the colour and light of the rays touches areas of pain and suffering.

You can use these healing rays in your own life by calling on I, Sanat Kumara to guide the rays of light into your home, family and community. I will work with you to raise the vibration of your light by directing these rays of transformation into all aspects of you and your world.

Affirmation
"I now give Sanat Kumara permission to transform and heal me, my family and my life with the healing rays of light."

Keywords: Bridge to Ancient Family, Healing Rays, Spiritual Father.

St Germain

I, St Germain have my fingers in many pies simultaneously! I work within the Galactic Councils to ensure humanity is prepared to move into a new vibration, to take a leap in consciousness and perceive things differently. I am involved in ensuring that each individual gets the most out of the many planetary alignments.

I take a global view in the development of this world. I see things from the perspective of one who has an overview of all things that are occurring on Earth in each moment. I have been involved in the Earth assignment for many eons and have always been a compassionate and understanding support to humanity. I have often incarnated upon Earth's floor and in my incarnations have endeavoured to be of service to the greater good. The work that I have contributed to humanity has always been for the purpose of awakening all to their highest possibility.

I now work with spiritual channels, performers and artists alike. I bring my message to humanity often through the arts and through the channelled writings of many. My role is to spread the word, to remind everyone of their true light and to aid the global Spiritual Family to unify through communication. I have always been strong on communication and have recognised its worth through my own lives on Earth and now through the lives of those I guide.

I do encourage humanity to love one another, to resolve disagreements through compassion and communication and to seek first the similarities in others rather than the differences. I have worked on Earth as a teacher and as an educator in many different capacities. I still offer this service to humanity and many 'take me up' on this offer by calling on me to assist them in their work and lives.

I am an advocate for the healing and transformational power of humour, laughter and comedy. I work in the day-to-day aspect of people's lives to bring in the lighter side. I am also a great support to those that endeavour to bring laughter into the lives of others through working in comedy or entertainment.

There is also a serious side to me in the sense that I care very deeply for our blessed Mother Earth and work very closely with those divine ones on Earth's floor committed to the conservation and preservation of the environment. Although there are many Nature Spirits that also work in this capacity, I very much support the conscientious movements of those dedicated to respecting the Earth and her naturally beautiful state. To all those that have ever planted even one tree, I do thank you, for your actions have blessed Mother Earth. I am a spiritual father to many aspects of Earth and thus I do care deeply for her healing and restoration. I thank all those that care with me. All my love to you all.

Please call on me often and I shall be with you always and forever.

Affirmation
"I call on the light-heartedness and spiritual humour of St Germain to enrich my spiritual path. I call on his divine assistance in all my endeavours."

Keywords: Spiritual Teacher, Divine Overseer of Earth, Inspiration, Laughter.

Quan Yin

I, Quan Yin am so pleased to be with you as I now talk of my responsibility in the development of humanity. I am most commonly known as the Goddess of Mercy within the Eastern traditions. This role sees me on many a Higher Council, bringing balance and compassion to many choices and decisions regarding human beings and their karma.

Because of my femininity many soldiers have come to me in times gone by. They have talked to me of their battles, their victories and their emotional losses. I have listened and have offered my solace and my heart, that is a sanctuary where the weary can rest. I have considered the positions of struggling men and have handed down my advice. I have been their counsel and their homes when they could not find their own within. I am a guiding light over dark lands and in dark times. I stand for mercy, forgiveness, equality, compassion, courage, strength and honour.

I have over the centuries been called upon by women of great courage and strength. They have sought my counsel in times of need where their path ahead is cloudy and misted over. I have brought to them my wisdom of the feminine ways, my understanding of womanhood and motherhood. My compassion has softened hearts that have grown hard through the harshness of life and its challenges. In this role I have been a teacher and have reminded women of the higher purpose of all things. This I have contributed to Earth out of my deep love for humanity.

My spirit crosses many lands; I see past, present and future. My heart can always be felt and sometimes heard. As you look to the sky, you may sense me stretched across it where I see many things but I always use this knowledge to love and guide you. People have been known to consult me on their life plan. Often they become excited when I come into their lives, for they know that I signify positive moves forward and the winds of light that bring change and opportunity.

You too can consult me of your life plan. Call on me and I shall work with you to understand your divine purpose on Earth in this life. I, Quan Yin am a mother to many and I shall stand by you silently at times and actively on other occasions always guiding, supporting and caring for you. Ask me to join you and I shall do.

Affirmation

"Dear Quan Yin, thank you for your constant support. Please assist me with your higher perspective. Show me the divine plan for my life. "

Keywords: Goddess of Mercy, Healing, Compassion, Life Plan.

Lord and Lady Lemuria

I, Lord Lemuria come forth this day to speak of one of my roles within the consciousness of humanity. I hold some of the frequencies that come together to create the Lemurian Consciousness. This Lemurian Consciousness is a most divine one indeed. I do love this energy for it is part of me. I am the masculine balance of the signature frequency that is the Lemurian Consciousness and I am equally balanced by my feminine aspect Lady Lemuria. Although we have many aspects of ourselves incarnated on Earth's floor in human form at this time, we exist as energy, as memory and as flow. We are the energy of purity and softness and the celestial gentleness of God. We are the divine sound of God when God is softly speaking. We are the tones of pale pink and baby blue, with a slight touch and shimmer of silver and gold. We are an energy.

Lemuria was a very giving, gracious and loving energy that manifested itself as a civilisation in a period prior to what you call your ancient history. Lemuria, although very real in a physical sense, was also ethereal in terms of lightness and multidimensional capacity. Its inhabitants were of the ability to move through realities and exist in many different dimensional experiences whilst maintaining a physical body. When we say 'physical body' however, we talk of physicality a lot lighter and more flexible than man's current human form. Over time bodies have changed. We anticipate that human bodies will become lighter once again as a result of being freed from the heaviness that negative thoughts and repressed emotions can bring.

The physical body of a Lemurian had the ability to maintain the age that was chosen by its owner. The body was able to transmute any abnormal cells, and was of the ability to be left for long periods of time, in a form of hibernation, giving its owner the opportunity to travel in spirit form in other dimensions and remain incarnated on Earth simultaneously.

We had many different species incarnated in Lemuria at the one time. These different species had different sexual expressions from each other. Some species experienced themselves as either male or female and others experienced themselves as both male and female. Even those in human form often chose to merge their masculine and feminine aspects as one, making them of one body rather than two separate expressions of the same soul.

Regardless of the sexual choices of a human being, each expression was considered equally valid in its own right. A human being chose its expression depending on its needs. If Lemurians wished to bear children, they would choose a female body. If the female chose to merge as one incarnation with her masculine balance, she would choose the 'one body'. Regardless of the chosen expression, it is important to remember that the bodies did not have a density like the bodies you live in now. Because these aspects did not have the density, they did not often have physicality in the form that you are used to. An 'of one body' expression, for example, may be a more ethereal manifestation where both male and female aspects step into their light bodies and merge as one body.

A 'light body' in the Lemurian sense was one that was not limited by the density of physical form and yet was still classified as a body for it had some form. The light body had many sacred centres, meridians, energy grids and fields of a physical body, yet did not have the solidity of physical matter. It was, however, possible to take on ones light body and still have a physical experience. Providing one still held the physical body (still lived on Earth), one could move from physical to light body, and back again. This was generally done in sleep, meditation, love making, ceremony, prayer and healing.

I, Lord and I, Lady Lemuria am here to assist all those who would like to communicate with us on matters of Lemurian history and the areas of light bodies, health and healing. We call forth all healers and physicians, and those aspiring to ascend upwardly to call upon us and instantly we shall be by your side to aid in all ways that we can. And thus is this now complete. *Amen, amen, amen.*

Affirmation
"Lord and Lady Lemuria, assist me to balance my life in the finer frequencies. Bless my life with healing. Elevate me to a higher state of being."

Keywords: Healing, Medicine, Health, Spiritual History, The Finer Frequencies, Joy, Relationships, Sexuality and Romance.

Lord and Lady Gaia

We, Lord and Lady Gaia are here today to send you our love and to talk a little about our role as the Spirit of the Earth. We are the light and essence of Earth's spirit and in our arms we hold Mother Earth and all of her children that are known as the Children of Earth. We can be understood as the spirit that runs through a heavenly body, we supply the light and the essence within Earth.

Earth is a combined project as so many Hierarchies came together to create it and so many have since populated it or have become involved in some way. We work closely with other beings such as the Essence of the Seas, Lord and Lady Neptune. We do however recognise it is difficult to understand that there could be a difference in the essences that come together to complete Earth.

Many people believe that Earth is one entity, Mother Earth, and she is a vast and body in her own right. This is correct in some respects, however Mother Earth is complex as she incorporated many other Hierarchies into her creation. For example, it is easy to look at a soccer ball and see it as one thing, however it is many things. It is stitching, stuffing, colour, leather, shape and feel. Now consider that all of these aspects come from different places. The leather came from a different home to the stuffing and stitching whereas the shape and feel are less tangible and came from a vision from someone else.

The Earth is like this. Although it works perfectly as one energy, the ocean's essence came from a different realm than the trees, and even then each tree comes from different areas within the galaxy. There was also a vision for the feel, shape and texture of Earth that was a shared vision of many. It was many eons ago that the Hierarchies combined to manifest their vision and thus was Earth created. Earth is still an essence in her own right, yet she co-exists with so many other essences.

Our role specifically is to fulfil the need for Earth to have a spirit. Every living entity must have a spirit, an energy that links the solid, physical form with All That Is, the Universal Life Force. We are an individual aspect of the Universal Life Force, as is the spirit within you. In truth at one level we are all the one energy but on other levels we have individuality within our life force and thus have we named our section of the universal life force, Lord and Lady Gaia.

We contribute to the overall creation of Earth by casting an angelic, celestial light on the planet which allows its magical and heavenly feel. There are certain areas on Earth that feel other-worldly and you have experienced some of these. Can you remember feeling as though you have walked into a completely different realm, and you have interrupted a party that was teeming with mystical life of fairies and spirits you can't quite see? We help create this feel on Earth with our angelic and celestial spirit. It is our energy that opens the corridors for other beings from kingdoms far away to visit Earth and to stay awhile.

We work closely with our beloved brother and friend Lord Pan. He, when Earth was created, was instrumental in building an environment compatible with the Angelic and Elemental Beings associated with the Nature Realms. Many trees refused to populate Earth without the support of the Beings of

Light that live in the forests and parks and tend to the wildlife, birds, plants and trees.

Lord Pan understood that in future times the Earth would need an excess of nature spirits to deal with the growing demands on the natural world to transmute poisons and to house wildlife that were fast losing their homes. He recognised that the nature spirits would also aid in keeping the morale high within the natural world amongst the damage and destruction. He also knew that humans who were close to the natural world would come to rely on the nature spirits to give them strength in times of darkness and despair. So far, Lord Pan has been right. Humans and the natural world have come to rest in the supportive arms of the nature spirits in order to regain their faith and continue on in their plight to aid in the Ascension of Mother Earth and humanity.

We, Lord and Lady Gaia help to create a stable and consistently loving environment on Earth for all of our helpers – whether they be in human, animal, plant or energetic form, by casting our spirit and its light into the hearts of all that accept us. We are thankful for each and every soul upon Earth's floor and we look forward to the day when all of creation choose to live harmoniously. We are thankful for the foresight of our Spiritual Family such as Lord Pan and our Earth Family. We have seen wise people on Earth populate land with trees that shall shelter many life forms, some forms unseen. Although the gifts these people have given many through the planting of even a single tree are priceless, we endeavour to show our appreciation through the love that we bestow upon such Earth and nature servers.

We take this opportunity to thank all those beloved ones that have aided Mother Earth, whether it be through the planting of trees or saving the natural environment by recycling or picking up rubbish. In recent years we have witnessed humanity come up with the most inspiring ideas to preserve and conserve the natural world. Some of these ideas individuals have remembered from their travels in past lives on other planetary worlds, and others are fresh ideas invented in this life. We are truly blessed to have such a motivated and innovative team of Earth servers. We thank all of you for your service. *Amen, amen, amen.*

Affirmation
"Lord and Lady Gaia, teach me to connect to the Earth and create a loving friendship with her. Assist me to develop the desire and commitment to truly look after and nurture Mother Earth."

Keywords: Environment, Earth Healing, Nature Spirits, Spirit of Earth, Angelic, Celestial Light.

Lord and Lady Tansafarie

Know too Dear Ones that we, Lord and Lady Tansafarie are now here today to discuss our role in the Spiritual Hierarchy for Earth. I, Lady Tansafarie support those who are the holders of the circle. I support those men and women who lead groups of people into inner levels of themselves. I support those that create the rituals of light for initiations and to symbolise important events. I can always be called upon to be of assistance at these times. Rituals may include a wedding ceremony, the christening of a child, a funeral, the Native American traditions of Sweat Lodge and Pipe Ceremony. I and my masculine balance support the rituals of monks, village people and the Westerners alike in their traditions for we recognise the importance of allowing some things to be treasured and acknowledged as sacred.

We also aid you to recognise the divine in the mundane. The sacred energy of a simple task once experienced can bring bliss. We balance the energy between the times of great significance and the times of daily routine. When one can come to understand their equality and to cherish and enjoy both equally, happiness can be achieved. We endeavour to bring these lessons to humanity so that they can come to understand the true gift Earth living is. You will get to a stage, if you haven't already, where you remember to stop and smell a rose or feel fresh ocean air, because it is not in every realm or on every planet that these things can be experienced. Earth is a special place for it is the home of so many unique and diverse experiences.

Many Human Incarnates rush through their days without realising there have been thousands of priceless situations where they had an experience and yet barely noticed it at all. We understand that many of you are very busy on Earth's floor and have chosen Earth assignments of difficulty where it can sometimes feel like a juggling act to get everything done. We only ask that you realise that sometimes the very thing you have been striving for comes along and because you are not experiencing life, you miss it. Other times it comes in and you say, "Great, I've achieved that" and then you move on to the next thing without really experiencing the gift of such an achievement.

It is important to bask in your successes and remind yourself of the importance of acknowledgement and ritual in your life. Sometimes the ritual can be the acknowledgement and the acknowledgement can be the ritual. Take time out to contemplate where you have been and how far you have come. Acknowledge yourself by recording certain events in a journal or on film. Experience yourself achieving and fulfilling your dreams and goals that you set in this life and also set many centuries ago. You can be a wonderful example to others on how to live, to give, to be. Allow yourself to shine in this truth and as your light shines, you encourage others to allow theirs to shine alongside yours.

We of the Tansafarie Hierarchy have also had great input into the establishment, spiritual development and growth of many indigenous peoples on Earth. Many of these ones do not originally come from Earth as their ancient people came from planets and systems far away. They volunteered to settle here to create a belief and value system for future civilisations to live by. Most of this has now been achieved. Humanity live by, and have access to, a higher level of awareness about the purpose and value of life due to valuable lessons and levels of information stored on Earth vibrationally and physically by the indigenous peoples. Some of the indigenous peoples chose to hide a lot of their sacred files in the energetic fields of sacred spaces and places such as Holy Mountains, lakes and rivers and most definitely in rocks, caverns and caves.

Rocks hold sacred wisdom as the rock medicine has the ability to store memories and ancient files. These files are not always in physical form like your files on Earth but they are still storehouses of information nonetheless. Those with the gift of reading the sacred files can sit beside a rock and listen carefully. Information will be given to the seeker according to what is appropriate. The record keeper (the rock for example) discerns this with the assistance of the seeker's Higher Self. Many of the Shamans or wise men and women of the village/tribe in times gone by could stand or sit beside the rock, cavern or cave and receive information about past history that was relevant to the village/tribe's current plight.

The wise person has always known that humanity has never been left to fend for itself, not even in times where it has been hard to see or sense much light on the planet. Earth has always contained the answers within itself, in the rocks, the crystals, the caverns and the caves. The indigenous people anchored sacred information here on Earth. Indigenous peoples placed sacred encodings of energetic and vibrational information into the rocks and sacred areas of Earth to be accessed at a later time.

You of pure heart can sit quietly in places of intense light and spiritual connectedness and listen carefully. You, in time, will hear the whisperings of the internal voice of the Earth and the rocks and crystals that are of Earth. You shall experience the wisdom for yourself and it shall embrace you as you integrate it into your daily living and through your service in the world.

When an individual or group chooses to tap into this information, all they need to do is put the intention forth and the wisdom shall connect and flow automatically to the one/s requesting it to do so. Often one person can ask for many people in the form of prayers for world peace. When an individual asks for his brothers, sisters and himself to learn about how to achieve community or world peace, the information and keys are released vibrationally for all who are willing to receive them.

You can call on the highest levels of information yourself to be made available to humanity so they may grow and expand to serve their highest good. The information can never be forced on an individual; however, by praying for it you ground a higher frequency into the consciousness of humanity. When an individual or group of people are ready to, they can easily access higher levels of awareness. These levels have already been established in the consciousness, patiently awaiting acceptance and an invitation into humanity's mind.

Individuals can be prepared to make a shift in attitude, perception and belief even though they are not consciously aware of what is happening. Due to energetic and spiritual information travelling vibrationally, higher levels of consciousness are more able to reach an individual's mind when it is relaxed. Having a relaxed mind makes it more susceptible to ideas and vibrations of a higher frequency. Energetic and spiritual information (higher frequencies) can visit people in dreams and in meditation. A person's Higher Self can utilise these important times to open the mind to higher frequencies to prepare the individual for an awakening.

I, Lord and I, Lady Tansafarie recognise the importance of having these higher levels of awareness available and thus do we support and assist the preservation of ancient texts already on Earth and the anchoring of new levels of information to reach humanity through ways of channelling, divine guidance and visions. We are here to support you as you connect to information already here and information now connecting to Earth in these current times. *Amen, amen, amen.*

Affirmation
"Lord and Lady Tansafarie, bless me with your knowledge of sacred ritual. Assist me to integrate this knowledge into my life. Aid me to tap into the divine mystery of life."

Keywords: Acknowledgement, Ritual, Recognition of the Sacred, Ceremony, Indigenous Peoples, Pathways to Ancient Information.

Lord and Lady Israel

Know too Dear Ones that I, Lord and I, Lady Israel will now speak to all of you of our role in assisting humanity at these moments in time.

Dear Ones, we are involved in many peace keeping roles. We have assisted in establishing many peace keeping organisations and movements upon Earth's floor. Peace keeping has many roles in the way we perceive it, for peace keeping can extend as far as addressing stresses that affect the individual, that in turn may affect the community and then the world. We are involved in peace keeping operations that are of a military nature as well as a charitable nature. We support Light-Workers that have assignments in military organisations, political organisations and the Red Cross.

We offer our support, wisdom, advice and love only for purposes of serving the highest good and will of humanity. Our desire is to see the healing of humanity's need to create pain and suffering. We have no political or power agenda of our own, only to see all return to self-empowerment and inner peace.

Assisting the individual to seek and find what brings contentment has been of the utmost importance to us. We have operated on the understanding that the outer conflict in the world is the extension of inner pain in the individual. It has been our intention to assist humanity to address the root cause of this inner pain.

We ask questions of humanity:
- What brings the individual pain?
  - Contemplate the causes of your pain.

After you have done this, consider:
- What brings humanity pain, collectively?

We that are of the Israel Hierarchy have studied the energy of pain and its causes for many centuries. We have researched it and have tested our theories through our own incarnations and the incarnations of all of you, our Spiritual Family.

It is our task to assist in alleviating pain and suffering and we have chosen to do this in the following four ways:

Acknowledgement

Our first way is through acknowledgement, encouraging humanity to consider pain, to understand it and then to seek to find its cause. Through this alone, pain loses its power over humanity for it is no longer denied or hidden in the cupboard. Explore the things that hold you back. Are there any instances from your past that still bring you pain or discomfort? Are there things from your past that can be healed and released now in order to set you free? Anything can be healed if you confront it within yourself, thus stripping it of its self-defeating power. There are many different ways to do this such as journal writing, joining a support group, meditation, and personal training such as seeking assistance from a counsellor or personal development facilitator. A very effective way is simple contemplation; sitting quietly and getting to know yourself. This becomes very powerful particularly if you intensify it in the beginning by sitting in nature or meditating with others on the same path.

Communication

The second way is through communication; development of sharing one's troubles with others through communicating burdens and fears. For many centuries humanity chose not to communicate honestly or at all about feelings. This choice brought even more pain through misunderstanding and isolation. Humanity experienced loneliness because communication (in ALL its forms) builds bridges between people. Without communication, bridges are not built and humanity experiences itself as separate and lonely. We have endeavoured to educate humanity about the importance of communication and with the Spiritual Hierarchy's assistance, have encouraged humanity to embrace communication and recognise its value beyond servicing basic needs.

Connection

The third way is through connection. We use the keys and gifts of communication and education to connect people to people. It is our intention to assist humanity to desire to know each other. This has been challenging as there have been many blocks to this built over time. The history of Earth gives humanity many examples to encourage them not to trust and yet there are so many on Earth that have ignored this and continue to hold the light for all. Ignorance and a belief in difference have separated brothers and sisters of humanity. Many have believed that men are different in essence to women and certain races are different to others in ways that make one superior to the other. In truth, all are one, all are equal. We have worked hard to educate those who, to protect themselves against their own fear, believe in inequality. We have worked to teach them to embrace unity and release the burdens of their beliefs. There have been many changes across Earth in recent years and we can see subtle shifts in humanity's psyche. We are anticipating that these subtle shifts will continue to grow and expand.

Action

The fourth way is through action. This is where our interest in organisations such as the Red Cross, child welfare groups and communities of people who involve themselves in the protection of animals and nature comes from. We support those who put their desire for peace into action by choosing to manifest changes in their physical world. We support those organisations that are honest, good and true and uphold the value and belief in peace. We hold the energy for those who often feel challenged as they struggle to make a difference in areas of great pain and suffering and we support them on the occasions when they lose faith in their mission.

> ***Affirmation***
> *"Lord and Lady Israel, I beckon you assist me to transcend any pain and suffering in my life. I ask you to assist in transcending the cycles of pain and suffering in humanity."*

Keywords: Peace Keeping, Organisations, Charity, Communication, Releasing Pain and Suffering.

Mother Mary

I, Mother Mary have been of service to myself, my Spiritual Family and humanity over many centuries. Each and every soul upon Earth's floor receives my heart love and appreciation.

I do appreciate the contribution of everyone on Earth, for collectively we are assisting in the ascension of the whole – every human, every inch of Earth and every realm above, below and within Earth itself. I aid specifically the humanitarian heart within every individual. I aid the growth of love for humanity in the individual and assist in dispersing feelings such as distrust, betrayal and anger. Those destructive belief systems of self-hatred, self-doubt and internal anger toward self, I also aid in transmuting. I work closely with those who give to themselves through giving to others.

I work on many Higher Councils and in turn aid those who sit on the Earth councils endeavouring to make positive change in community, society, government and humanity. I often involve myself in the training of those who, throughout their life, shall be servers of humanity. I work with those endeavouring to bring about great change. As a healer of many wounds, I train those desiring to be healers to also heal the great heart wounds in others and thus do I head many sacred healing temples and councils existing in the Higher Realms.

I am not always 'the Boss' my dears, for that may be what it seems! I support as much as I lead. I am not always the one out front; more often I work behind the scenes. I have had many incarnations where I have worked silently in service to myself and humanity, but always my energy has been available at a higher level as a guiding light for others. I come now to offer my service to you individually to improve your relationships with the children and adults in your life. I come to aid marriages, relationships, partnerships and family dynamics. I come to aid you to open a new level of your family and humanitarian heart and develop strong bonds of love. Old fears of abandonment and loneliness can transmute now and only love, care and kindness exist.

I develop the trust in families, in women and in men. Have faith, I am now here to aid. Love and peace can now reign in your heart, the heart of your family and those around you in a social and community sense. *Amen, amen, amen.*

Affirmation
"Dear Mother Mary, please bless my family with your love, care and support. Teach me to live in love and help me heal my family through unconditional love and divine light."

Keywords: Family, Community, Global Connectedness, Healing, Service, Charity.

The Celtic Lord of the Forests

I am Lord of the Forests of a sacred area within the Celtic vibration and region. I roam the forests within the lands that I speak of. I am a Light Being whose intention is to serve Earth as Earth has served me. I have encountered many beings in my centuries upon Earth. Some are human and they have seen me, but more often I connect with animals, nature spirits and of course the spirits of the trees. I can now admit to fears that have surfaced in me over the past century. For although I see all things, past and future, I have been prone to uncertainty in regard to the will of humanity to treasure this sacred planet of Earth.

I listen to the words of the wise ones that have spoken over time. I am reminded that it is vital to restore my faith in humanity for humanity in truth is among the most gentlest of breeds. Humanity has forgotten their true nature in some respects and as a result has acted in ways that are not their true nature. It is we of the Higher Beings that see all, that must maintain our love, respect and trust in humanity for it is through this that they shall remember their true essence and nature.

I thank you for this opportunity to speak and I remind all Light Beings that I am available to talk to if they do choose. It is for them to simply enter into meditation and beckon me and I shall present myself energetically, visually or verbally. *Amen, amen, amen.*

How to Connect with the Celtic Lord of the Forests

- Sit in a place that is comfortable, preferably in nature, leaning against a tree.
- Close your eyes and feel the warmth and strength of the tree against you.
- Breathe gently as you begin to sense a presence near you.
- This presence is the Celtic Lord of the Forests.
- Ask this presence to stand in your energy field to protect you and connect you to the natural world. Feel the Celtic Lord's presence even more strongly.
- Ask him, "What can I do to best connect to the natural world?"
- Listen carefully. You may intuitively receive the answer or hear it as a voice of light in your mind. You may also receive a picture or vision.
- Know that the Celtic Lord will return to you when you fulfil tasks that have been suggested.
- Extend your gratitude to him for assisting you. You may wish to spend more time in his presence, communicating further before you return.
- To return, breathe deeply and slowly open your eyes.

Affirmation
"I allow the Celtic Lord of the Forest to aid me to restore my faith in humanity and to connect me to the natural world."

Keywords: Faith, Connection, Celtic Forests, Mystery and Magic.

Lord and Lady Avalon

We are indeed the essence of a consciousness that has intrigued, mystified and on occasion, frightened humanity. Our light was never designed to create fear; it was designed to be accessible to all. As the energies now shift on the planet, this is becoming a reality. Our light is indeed flowing forth for many to receive, and for this, we are greatly pleased.

Many have spent time within our higher halls and councils of great wisdom. These are held in realms known consciously by some upon Earth's floor, but unknown to many. It is in these Higher Councils and halls of great experience and learning that much sacred training is conducted, many important choices are made and aspects of humanity's welfare is overseen.

We, Lord and Lady Avalon and our divine council are truly honoured to once again connect to those in human incarnation who desire our assistance and access to our love, abilities and wisdom. We are here to welcome all into our Great Halls of Learning, Love and Light. The mysteries of our vibration are indeed now open to more individuals than before and we welcome those wishing to be initiated into the Avalon consciousness.

Our vibration connects strongly to the natural world, the elements, the animals, the sacred waters and the spirits within Earth. This is not to say however that our vibration is only of Earth for we are an Ancient Energy that has planted seeds in many civilisations and cultures in ancient lands and realms not of Earth. We have travelled far to be here and have been on Earth's floor since the initial grounding of the Lemurian consciousness into Earth's vibration. We and our Avalonean team are now available as a bridge to bring humanity home to this ancient energy; the Ancient Energy of Avalon, Lemuria and even to the purest aspects of Atlantis.

We are here to initiate those devoted ones into a new level of spiritual and philosophical awareness, whilst attaining an even deeper connection with the divine Nature Realms of this planet and all other realms and lands that we have planted our seeds of light within. Our seeds, planted in Earth many thousands of years ago, are now beginning to awaken, flourish and grow. It is an exciting time for us as the awakening of these most sacred seeds of knowledge, wisdom and spiritual technology will awaken pure, spiritual memory banks within the humans that allow it to be. Once these memory banks activate, those individuals will begin to remember their true and ancient selves.

If you are drawn to us it may be because of these sacred keys of light, these seeds of purity awakening in you as they are in Mother Earth. To assist the process, allow yourself to meditate upon the highest levels of the ancient consciousness that has come to aid humanity. Ask your Higher Self to raise your awareness to a higher vibration of light, colour and sound and it shall be done.

I, Lady Avalon do come forth to remind you of my feminine light that is also accessible. Thus do I come forth in the forms of all things feminine to encourage you to embrace, appreciate, and recognise your own beauty and unique light. It is my divine honour to be upon Earth's floor in spirit and essence at this crucial time of reconnection and reawakening. I encourage you to reconnect to the consciousness of Avalon for it shall enrich your heart and mind.

Avalon in essence is a cradle, a haven, a village of light for healers, magicians, spiritual teachers and students. It is a melting pot of the mystical and mythical. All levels of alchemy are understood here; the alchemy of the heart, mind and body as well as the physical realms. Avalon is equally balanced in its masculine and feminine energy and does support the unity of the both. It does not exclude one and glorify another. Avalon is a home to priests and priestesses, Gods and Goddesses, males and females alike. It has always been this way and will continue to be.

Many associate Avalon with the creation of many sisterhood rituals or rites. This is a correct association, for Avalon is in favour of the unity of the feminine vibration in the form of the Sisterhood Council. Avalon has also been known to host many sacred events centred around the bridging of the Sisterhood to the Brotherhood, and sometimes honouring the Brotherhood in its own right, absent of the Sisterhood.

Avalon is a celebration through sacred rites of the essence of masculinity and femininity. So join us within our sacred halls. Close your eyes gently and go to a safe place. I, Lord and I, Lady Avalon will meet you here and we shall take you to our special places in your meditation journey. We shall introduce you to our Halls of Learning and peaceful Garden of Light, and you shall be forever blessed with the experience of our love and light. You can then return to us whenever you wish and we will be with you to guide, aid, and love you.

Both I, Lord and Lady Avalon do send our love to you and we remind you that we are always beside you, indeed. *Amen, amen, amen.*

Affirmation
"Lord and Lady Avalon, I allow myself to enter into the sacred Halls of Learning with you. I allow the sacred mysteries of Avalon to enrich and raise the spiritual vibration of my life."

Keywords: Great Learning, Initiation, Knowledge Through Love, Equality, Structural and Institutional Support.

Lord and Lady Jerusalem

I, Lord and I, Lady Jerusalem am now here to assist to reconnect you to the true heart and inner core of your Higher Self. You exist not only in human form, but also as part of a multidimensional system known as a Spiritual Hierarchy. Our task is to reacquaint you with your heart which lives within the core of your Spiritual Hierarchy. When you become more connected to your Hierarchy's core and heart, you begin to grow in compassion, understanding and a true desire to alleviate your own suffering and the suffering of others. You begin to reawaken your deepest humanitarian aspects and find yourself receiving untold joy and inner gifts through being of assistance to others.

We are here to help you reawaken into these aspects of you. Once they are completely reawakened they may begin to steer you into occupations or volunteer work where you can truly aid others. You may desire to plant trees, clean up waterways, or simply be there for someone who needs a hand. Humanity must work together to free itself collectively and individually. You may strengthen in your desire to go within and find your personal power. You may embark upon a personal/spiritual development journey that shall take you into truly knowing yourself. As you truly come to know yourself, you are in a stronger position to unconditionally help others. This journey that I, Lord and I, Lady Jerusalem now take with you is one where you shall first come to know yourself and then know yourself through your service to yourself and to others.

In this process it is as important to receive as it is to give. Allow yourself to receive the blessings of the Spiritual Hierarchy for Earth as they now shower you with love, assistance and great teachers as you work your way systematically through this new level of development. We thank you for joining our team. Know that you can volunteer however you choose. Every contribution is appreciated. You will not be forced into everything! Every little bit you give is one step closer to our collective achievement of inner peace, family peace and world peace. We are here to connect you upwardly, inwardly and outwardly so that you may receive the training from the Higher Realms to be on the physical plane what we call a Light-Worker.

As a Light-Worker you are here to anchor the Light for and into humanity in any way you choose. Whether you choose to be a world leader, a lecturer, a nurse, a mother, or a farmer we are thankful for your equal contributions. Light-Workers are needed in all areas of life. We, Lord and Lady Jerusalem do oversee the Councils of Light-Workers upon Earth with many other Beings of Light, and are here to aid, support, guide and counsel you. Let us truly assist you now.

If you have lost your way, not sure of what to do or are torn between two worlds, call on us. We shall shine the light on the highest path you can take. We shall light your heart so that you can know yourself and recognise the divinity that lives within. If you doubt your own light and purity, call upon us and we shall clarify these worries in your mind so that you can know your true light that always shines brightly. We shall send you the signs so that you know this to be true.

We are here to renew your faith and trust in yourself as a divine Light-Worker for humanity and Earth. We are here to help you reach deeper levels of yourself so that you may know your own light. We are here to clear illusions about what you may fear yourself to be. If you doubt your Light, and fear that you are not worthy, these illusions, we shall clear. We are here to aid you to open your heart deeply unto yourself and to then express this heartfelt love onto others. Allow us to work with you. Remember that you are always welcome on our team. Thank you for your light, your love, and your contribution to humanity. *Amen, amen, amen.*

Affirmation
"I now call upon Lord and Lady Jerusalem to support, guide and teach me to discover deeper levels of myself and then share

these newly discovered gifts with others. Please reconnect me to the Light-Workers team and councils and connect human Light-Workers to me now so that I can feel more supported in my physical life."

Keywords: Heart, Compassion, Humanity, Light-Workers.

Lord and Lady Maitreya

Know too Dear Ones that I, Lord and I, Lady Maitreya will now come forth and talk about our role in the Spiritual Hierarchy for Earth. Although we have many spiritual functions we shall focus on a small section of our work as it relates directly to humanity.

I, Lady Maitreya am here to establish the feminine principle within the businesses of Earth. Until fairly recently business has been primarily based on masculine energy. This is now balancing itself to include the jewels of business that can be offered by the feminine. The feminine principle is the divinely creative, intuitive, nurturing, caring and maternal energy that supports and gives to Earth and humanity.

Men and woman are becoming empowered as the feminine energy that lives within them awakens. Many have feared in the past that too much feminine energy in business would destroy the essence of business as it would create too much of a softening and flow. These fears are being transmuted and women now move forth in the world contributing the feminine principle to many business endeavours.

I, Lady Maitreya come to assist to empower the feminine element within the business world as well as the feminine energy within every man. I am a strength and support to all those who are self-taught and to all those who have had a dream and against all odds have seen this dream manifest. I am an advocate for all those that desire to push their creativity into the business world and for their creativity to inspire and enliven others. I am here today to motivate and inspire all those trying in a competitive world to hold fast to their dreams so that their dreams carry them to contentment through the doorway of their success. Allow I, Lady Maitreya to assist you for I shall work with you in the world and then balance you in your private life and internal sanctuary.

I stand beside my masculine partner and balance Lord Maitreya. Together we are One among many that ground the Light of Christ into humanity. We are here today to ground this light into you and to have it inspire and guide you. Trust in this light that guides you. Trust in this light that comes through your Hierarchy and through all Hierarchies. Every being upon Earth's floor can be an initiate of the Christ training so that they too may be a Christ Light to ground Christ Consciousness into humanity.

If you have the desire to take on this higher spiritual training, call upon us, Lord and Lady Maitreya and we shall come to you. We shall watch over you as you leave your body at night time. We shall join with you as your spirit travels to the sacred halls of other realms. We shall train you in this state and when you return to your body in the morning you shall feel inspired by a higher light and a new but familiar feeling you can't quite explain. It is on these mornings you shall know that you have spent the night with us, training to be a Christ Light. This Christ Light shall lift your awareness over time from third dimensional perspectives into the fifth dimensional framework. It is here that you shall discover many new abilities such as intuitive/ psychic awareness and healing gifts. You shall also feel a strong sense of connectedness with the divine.

So call upon us, Lord and Lady Maitreya and we shall work with you either within a business capacity or within a Christ Light training capacity, or both. On a business level we shall assist to inspire you and anchor higher spiritual principles into your business philosophy, your creations and your practical plans. We shall encourage you to allow abundance in your life and will counsel you in difficult times. Allow us to be of assistance in this way and you shall feel divinely supported and cared for in all that you do.

On a Christ Light training level, we shall take you by the hand and walk you into a new world of spiritual understanding and ability. You shall remember valuable skills lying dormant within you from previous incarnations and other times. You will use these skills to facilitate your own healing, and the healing of others, as humanity collectively ascends into higher levels of awareness, which is the Christ Consciousness within. Open your heart to us and in this next phase we shall divinely guide you through this process.

I, Lord Maitreya have many roles in my service to humanity. I am here to offer insights to Light-Workers that call on me. My insights are of wisdom and based on many eons of experience and connection. I am a spiritual elder and as a result often take on the role as a spiritual grandfather, mentor or teacher to initiates. I have come to Earth many times in an effort to release humanity from the confines of old and limiting beliefs into higher levels of awareness and perception. Humanity is now at a stage in evolution where it is ready to embrace higher levels of consciousness. It is now that I am most useful for I have been entrusted with a task to shift the consciousness of humanity by releasing higher keys of spiritual insight into groups of people at certain important times on Earth such as planetary alignments, time and moon cycles. At key times on Earth I harness the opportunity to ground higher vibrations into the psyche, consciousness and energy fields of Earth and the global family.

I can be called upon by anyone at any time and will always respond. In meditation I often come to those who ask, as a soft warm slightly golden light and a feeling of strength and comfort. Some have seen me come as a lion for in this way I represent courage of heart, loyalty and strength. Although I can shape-shift into many forms, I do admit to coming to people in dreams and meditation in the lion form. On occasion I have been known to fly as eagles do and have visited my initiates in this form to remind them that they too can fly, they too can see the overview. I remind them of the wisdom and ability of the eagle, for although the eagle can see the overview it keeps its eye on the smallest of details and vice versa.

I have very strong connections to the Brotherhood of Light, a council that has held the energy for humanity for many centuries. Here I sit as a Divine Overseer and ensure that all goes according to plan for humanity. I can often be sensed by initiates as a force of golden light within the Himalayan Mountains.

I am part of the Christ Consciousness on Earth's floor and have taught these higher principles and mysteries for many centuries. Call upon me to direct and aid you in the reconnection of your human self to the higher levels of you. I shall aid you to bridge home to the ever wise ancient aspect of you, your eternal self that rests in the gentle, silent heart of this galaxy. *Amen, amen, amen.*

Affirmation
"I now open my heart and mind to Lord and Lady Maitreya. May they bless me with their light as they educate, train and care for me. Amen, amen, amen."

Lady Maitreya Keywords: Motivation, Business Minds, Initiation, Feminine Empowerment, Christ Light Training.

Lord Maitreya Keywords: Spiritual Teacher, Ancient Wisdom, Christ Consciousness, Brotherhood of Light.

Lord and Lady Neptune

Know too Dear Ones that I, Lord and I, Lady Neptune will come forth and speak of our roles in the Spiritual Hierarchy for Earth and in assisting humanity. We have many roles within the Oceanic and Neptunian departments of the Spiritual Hierarchy for Earth. We oversee the developments in the maintaining of and the harmony within all aspects of the oceans, bays and seas of Earth as well as the flow of energy from these areas to and from the planet Neptune. We are dedicated to the maximum performance of this system as the oceanic areas of Earth and their connections with Neptune bring many blessings and gifts to humanity.

There are other planetary worlds with their various oceans and seas that we are also involved in and oversee, however these are not yet fully relevant to humanity. There will come a time when humanity is ready to learn and be actively involved in the workings of these other planetary worlds and will work alongside kingdoms not of Earth, to find solutions, discuss ideas and plan the future. Humanity will also understand the role the Spiritual Hierarchy for Earth has had in servicing not only Earth but sister kingdoms also.

Aside from our roles off-planet, we share many gifts with humanity on a regular, day-to-day basis. We can be of great assistance to all those who have chosen to bring forth healing to others in the form of Reiki, hands-on healing, faith healing and the Laying on of Hands etc. We can be beckoned to restore the allowing and flowing of the feminine balance found in oceanic energies, to the individual. Just as the tides roll in and out, so can this gentle flow of allowing all to simply be, be restored in humanity.

Those that are desperately trying to control their circumstances or who are anxious, uptight and are fearing change can be relieved through allowing the gentle flow to return to their bodies and minds. The position of the sand and water changes continually. Joy comes from allowing this natural rhythm in your life as the flow of it brings peace. For all healers working with those who are frightened to let go, call upon us, Lord and Lady Neptune, and we shall aid you.

To all those who sing and use their voices to heal themselves and others, call upon us and we shall send forth sounds from deep within the mysterious heart of the oceans of Earth. These sounds shall reach you telepathically and as you allow your voice to fly, thus shall the most inspiring and magical sounds come from your mouth, lifting and healing others. Trust in these tones that can heal on a multidimensional scale, and thus shall you be surprised by the miracles in healing that can occur.

For those who desire deeper connection to the Spiritual Hierarchy for Earth, call upon I, Lord and I, Lady Neptune and we shall create a bridge that shall unify you with your own Higher Self. We shall come to you at night time as you sleep and place our healing hands upon you. Our light shall work into the mind, body and heart of you to restore you to your true light. Call upon us and we shall aid you to be all that you can truly be in this life. We shall teach you about your Spiritual Family, developing your confidence and trust to connect to your higher ancient lineage that is and has always been a deep and true part of you.

Allow we, Lord and Lady Neptune to reunite you with many aspects of your Higher Self and family. With your permission we will begin working with you immediately. *Amen, amen, amen.*

Affirmation
"I beckon the energies of divinity of Lord and Lady Neptune into me. May they connect me to the Oceanic Family of Light. May they assist me in every way so that I may be all that I am truly meant to be."

Keywords: Spiritual Family, Singing, Oceanic Healing Gifts, Healing, Allowing, Flow.

Lord and Lady Amphibian

Know too Dear Ones, I, Lord and I, Lady Amphibian will now explain our role within the Spiritual Hierarchy for Earth. We are the balance between land and sea, wet and dry, and all things that shape-shift and change in order to be compatible with both of these worlds. We also stabilise emotions within our realms and also within those Hierarchies that call upon our unique assistance.

We stabilise the emotional energies in those human beings that awaken to their spiritual journey and begin to reconnect home to the Spiritual Hierarchy for Earth. There are many who are awakening and reconnecting to the higher spiritual realms after spending many Earth-years shut down from this higher energy. When they begin to remember all that they have forgotten, all old emotions rise to the surface to make way for the new higher emotions of joy and happiness.

We are here to assist in cleansing away old emotions and bring up emotional deposits that may be locked in the body as past pain. We clear the emotional body of all residue and begin integrating the higher levels of the emotional body to bring in joy and happiness. As this process unfolds we stabilise the energy between the resurfacing of old emotions, the cleansing of the emotional body and the integrating of the higher emotional body. All this is done through us, Lord and Lady Amphibian as you begin to awaken. Sometimes the awakening process can be a frightening and an unstable time for people upon Earth's floor. It is the unknown territory they begin to move into, as well as the sudden awareness of the reality they have been living in, that can be shocking and emotionally devastating for some.

Some of our beloved children begin to awaken and thus realise the great pain they have been subjecting themselves to through the circumstances and lifestyles they have chosen. Others begin to realise that they may have steered themselves in a direction that contradicts how they really feel. All these things we are here for and can work towards healing. Not all will go through the emotional devastation of awakening. There will be those that shall quietly awaken, having small insights into themselves as they reconnect and experience times of hardship and times of peace. We too are with these ones as their emotional stability and to assist in the integration of their higher emotional body.

Remember it does not matter what method you use or how your emotional body chooses to cleanse itself. What is important is that your emotional body does make the choice to ascend. Call upon us, Lord and Lady Amphibian. Call upon our cleansing rains of love, light and healing and we shall dance within you and rid you of all that no longer serves you.

We are with you now for you are preparing to, or are in the process of, reconnecting and awakening to not only your Higher Self, but the Spiritual Hierarchy for Earth that is part of your Spiritual Family. Allow your emotions to flow as they need to, for in this flow healing occurs. Feel the joy as it dawns upon you that you are truly reconnecting home. Do not be afraid of your emotions whether you judge them as good or bad, they are simply the old levels clearing away from you to make way for the new.

Embrace this stage of your Ascension process, this reconnection phase, this new level of awakening. We that are of the Amphibian council and We Lord and Lady Amphibian are with you at this time. Do not doubt this. Look for our signs in the gentle rains, the ponds and pools of water and of course the frog medicine that we are a part of, and know that we are with you. Call upon us, give us permission to work with you and we shall do, continually.

Affirmation
"I call upon Lord and Lady Amphibian, to enter into me and to cleanse me, stabilise me and reconnect me to all that I truly am. Amen, amen, amen."

Keywords: Emotional Cleansing and Stabilising, Awakening, Reconnecting, Balance, Frog Medicine, Cleansing Waters, Rain.

Lord and Lady Sebastian

Dear One! We that are of the Jerusalem Hierarchy will come forward this day and introduce our beloved Lord Sebastian and his feminine balance Lady Sebastian.

Know too Dear Ones that We, Lord and Lady Sebastian come today to speak of our role within the Spiritual Hierarchy for Earth and our Spiritual Family.

We have not always taken a direct role and position with humanity as our work had kept us further away in the planetary grids, outer galactic and universal realms of this galaxy and beyond. We have now chosen to take a more direct approach with humanity and to begin with we will talk a little about our natures. We are highly fond of light heartedness, happiness, joy, humour, and kindness to all creatures, humans included! We are of an oceanic frequency which means we can shape-shift into various forms in order to fulfil our roles in oceans throughout this galaxy.

We have a rather large directorship role in terms of overseeing the balance within the seas and oceans. We direct all of the major movements, shifts and changes that occur within the oceanic worlds and endeavour to make sure everything runs smoothly. We belong to many councils and spend a lot of time travelling between different worlds. We have a strong interest in humanity at this time because its inner light has turned on. We have watched humanity from afar for many centuries and it is now that we have observed its light awakening and burning brighter by the day.

We have some of our team members on Earth's floor and if they do not know who they are, they are soon to remember. These ones are part of the Oceanic Hierarchy and vast Spiritual Family, the Sea and Oceanic Hierarchy. They may have their individual Hierarchies but their oceanic aspects come together to form the Oceanic Spiritual Family. It is very exciting for us to bring through this message for as we do, we send a telepathic call through the consciousness of humanity to awaken all those of our frequency.

In truth we are all of the same family however there are different sections to the family. There are sections belonging to the nature spirits and realms. These ones are of the woods and lakes and trees. There are the Earth Family members who are of the caves and fiery caverns of Earth, the rocks and mountains. Then there are the space beings who long for the stars and worlds of galactic vibrations. And of course there is our beloved Oceanic Family – the sea angels, star fish and all creatures and Beings of Light of the sea.

As we said before, in truth we are all one family. As a higher aspect of your Hierarchy you have aspects of yourself belonging to the Sea/Oceanic Family, the Nature Spirit/Realm Family, the Earth Family and the Outer and Intergalactic Family, for in truth you are all things. It is common to hold different aspects of yourself from various realms in your body simultaneously at different times in your life. You may also have an affinity with two or more realms because you remember your connectedness to all things. One aspect of you may know home as the woods, the other as the ocean.

Ultimately when all aspects of you return home from their travels through these homes and families, they return to the core of you, the heart of your Hierarchy. Here, home is a creation that combines the creativity, the energy, and the essence of every aspect of you, to manifest a realm and kingdom that is completely you, in your highest form. As you now begin to connect to your Hierarchy, it shall hold and teach you lovingly as it takes you on a step by step journey. Through the layers of the outer aspects of your realm you shall travel until you reach the heart of your Hierarchy, the very core of you. The beauty, the purity, the extraordinary colour, light, and sound of the magical masterpiece of the realm is all you, it is the essence of you and the creation that springs forth as an extension of you.

I, Lord and I, Lady Sebastian do encourage and hold the energy for you as you begin the journey consciously into the core/heart of your Hierarchy. We enjoy watching you delight in the pleasures that await you there and how they shall encourage your self-realisation as you understand your vastness. On reaching home you step into oneness and full and complete connectedness with the force and source of light that is God. I, Lord and I, Lady Sebastian stand beside you as you now take this path home into your true light and into the source of all light. *Amen, amen, amen.*

Affirmation

"Lord and Lady Sebastian, please connect me to the Galactic Realms beyond Earth. Please connect me to the vast spiritual network of Light Beings in the Higher Realms. Take me into the core of my being, the heart of my Hierarchy."

Keywords: Humour, Light Heartedness, The Realm of Home, Oceanic Frequencies.

Lord and Lady of the Lake

Dear One, I, Lord and I, Lady of the Lake stand beside you as you read this information. You may have heard of the Lady of the Lake from many fantasy novels of the Arthurian times. I am an energy of love and light that has worked with humanity for many centuries. I stand beside my masculine balance, the Lord of the Lake, and our existence holds great symbolism and meaning for humanity.

We are often like the 'young lovers' for we hold the energy of romance. We hold the energy for the special magic that flows between two human beings in love. We also hold the energy for romance, not just between two people, but between a person and life, life and nature, nature and people, the sun and the sea. For all things that can connect, we hold the keys to romance entering into that relationship.

Romance can be found in cooking a meal for loved ones, sewing a shirt or darning socks, gardening and growing flowers and herbs or simply sitting in the sunshine on a warm day. Allow the romance energy to enter into all that you do, and allow it to grace your heart and mind. Romance is a state of mind and heart, and can be abundant in your life whether you are in love with a partner, in love with life or with both. I, Lord and I, Lady of the Lake are of purity, divine romance and lightness and joy. Allow us to truly bless your life this day, and forevermore and thus shall your life begin to bloom, like a spring garden with the rewards that romance can bring.

Allow romance to enter into your life today. Telephone or write to people whom you really love and care for. Speak with them and thank them for their gifts, the gifts they bring to your life. If you cannot tell them this just yet, bring them a gift or service that can express your feelings without words. Make a meal, pot a plant for them or wash down their windows. Any way of showing appreciation has its own rewards. Watch your heart sing as you reach out to others.

Bring more romance into your life by playing music that lifts your spirits. Music and those that create it are a special gift from the heavens to humanity. Those special ones that write or perform music of love do so to truly elevate your mind, heart and spirit. Trust music in your life. Use it to bring the love of life into you.

Surround your home with gifts of the Earth. Fresh flowers, plants, rocks and herbs can adorn your home to reconnect you with your Mother Earth. Fish in ponds and wild birds bring great joy to your home. Allow these things to bless your life. Colours, sounds and light are all things that your body, mind and spirit need to shine and thrive. Allow these into your home and life.

I, Lord and I, Lady of the Lake can work with you to restore romance in your life and into your relationship if it is in some need of extra help and guidance. Relax and know that we are here to help you. If you are not in a relationship and would like to attract a supportive, caring and loving relationship, call on we and we shall get into action on it straight away! Clear the pathway for a partner by allowing yourself to express to us all of your fears and ways that you have felt hurt or believe you have hurt others in your past.

If you carry guilt, blame, self-blame, fear, shame and insecurity, call on us, and we shall work you through to the resolution of these issues. You can begin transmuting these feelings and fears through writing them out on a piece of paper. Be as honest with your writing as possible for then you will truly set yourself free. After you have spoken your heart's truth to us and to the page, surrender your fears by visualising us lifting the burdens of the past from you. To symbolise the shedding of the old, you may wish to burn the piece of paper.

We hold great wisdom in our heart and soul. This wisdom we can impart to you. We hold great magic in our fingers and this magic we can sprinkle into your life if you allow us to. Let us bring integrity, purity and true romance into your life today and forevermore. Speak to us about your inner dreams and we shall aid you to realise these.

Affirmation

"Dear Lord and Lady of the Lake, please bless my life with the romance energy. Help me to truly appreciate all aspects of life, even the most mundane tasks. Help me to see life's beauty and to experience joy and romance in all that I do, have and see. Allow me to flow with this reawakened love for life."

Keywords: Romance, Love of Life, Appreciation, Love.

Lord and Lady Savatar

Know too Dear One that We, Lord and Lady Savatar shall now come forth and speak to you. Our roles within the Spiritual Hierarchy for Earth are not so much on Earth as they are within the higher levels and dimensions not yet fully connected to humanity. We work within the planetary worlds that are of the Learians, the Syrians, the Pleiadians and do often travel to Andromeda and other such realities. Our work is more of a technological nature and we bridge different worlds through telepathic and frequency communications.

We use sound and the emanation of certain waves to allow sound to reach different parts of the galaxy. We also head many communication bays where information is gathered in bulk and sent to different areas of this galaxy. Such a process has most recently been used to assist Earth. Over the last twelve years (or since the early 1990s) great blocks of information have been sent to Earth to assist in the establishment of many new communication grids for humanity. As the computer internet hook up occurs on the physical plane, so does it occur on the higher levels for humanity.

Many members of your earthly kind have requested stronger, more supportive channel systems so that they can better communicate with higher levels of their higher selves and Incarnation Councils. Since these requests have been processed, we, Lord and Lady Savatar and all other members of our teams have been working to strengthen the channels of all those who consciously or unconsciously requested them to be so. Many people are now receiving stronger messages from their Higher Selves than ever before. They are receiving clear, concise guidance through a system that is strengthening every day.

We, Lord and Lady Savatar are here to work on the technical aspects of channelling and communication from above. We are here to ensure that your information comes through clearly, completely and in a language and level that you can understand. We team with other beings to phrase information in a way that triggers the sacred memory banks that are held in the cellular memories of your body. We work within the boundaries of your divine blueprint to ensure that all information you do receive does not affect the timing of the activation of new levels of awareness in you, from your blueprint. We work alongside many different Hierarchies and councils to develop and maintain an information and communication grid. This is so all members of our galaxy's community can be reached or can reach us through various forms of communication.

You can call upon us, Lord and Lady Savatar to work with you so that you may come to know and understand your unique communication system and where you fit into the communication grid of this galaxy. You may feel as though your channels are not strong or clear or that you do not have any accessible channels. In these cases, call upon we Lord and Lady Savatar and we will work with you to repair any areas that are not strong. We shall work to educate and train you to begin channelling and to use channels for your highest good and benefit. We shall assign you skilled Beings of Light who are 'channel technicians' that can help you to open up these parts of yourself. Allow yourself to grow in this area and know that we are here to guide you and support you in every way we can. We send our love and blessings to you and urge you to request our assistance when needed.

Affirmation
'I now allow Lord and Lady Savatar to assist me in every way to grow and learn about my place within the communication grids of this galaxy. May they open, clear and strengthen my channels so that I may communicate with the higher levels of myself at all times I choose to.'

Keywords: Communication, Channels, Technology, Galactic Grids.

How to Connect to the Beings of Light Supporting You

The Great White Hall

The Great White Hall is a meeting place for all Beings of Light and is always available to you to use as a place to heal and receive information. In your spiritual development, the Great White Hall can assist you to connect to your Higher Self and Guides. As you are aware, you can also use it for 'Aspect Therapy'.

The Great White Hall Meditation

- Visualise your spirit slowly lifting up and out of your body. From its new viewpoint, your spirit can see the whole room that your body is lying in.

- Your spirit floats up to the ceiling, through the roof, and to a height where you can see the rooftops of any local buildings.

- Moving higher up now, you begin to see not only your area, but also neighbouring suburbs or surrounding countryside.
- As you float higher and higher, you begin to feel as though you are moving out of the Earth's atmosphere.
- You can see Earth below as you move further out into the galaxy.
- You can feel the velvety blackness of the galaxy all around you.
- Up ahead you can see the shimmering lights of distant stars and worlds, however we are not going there today, we are going somewhere else...
- In the blackness of the galaxy, you can see not far from you, an outline of a door.
- The reason you can tell it is a door against the blackness of the galaxy is that the light from the realm on the other side of the door shines through it.
- Float over to the door and place your hand on the door handle.
- Gently open the door and step onto the lush green lawn of the realm you are now connecting to.
- Shut the door behind you and begin to walk across the lawn.
- Above you, you can feel the blueness of the sky, the warm sunshine on your face and ahead of you, and the gentle spray of mist from the water features that grace the garden.
- As you look ahead, beyond the water features, you see the magnificent and massive 'Great White Hall'. From the hall extends a fan of white marble steps.
- Allow yourself to walk towards the Great White Hall, drinking in its beauty and strength. You approach the steps.
- As you walk closer to the hall, you notice that its two massive entrance doors are opening slightly.
- A beautiful Being of Light steps out and stands on the marble steps.
- As you move closer you may notice certain characteristics.

- Is the Being of Light male or female or of no particular gender at all?
    - Does it wear or hold anything that may indicate its origins, culture or connections?
- Walk closer to this Being of Light.
- Sit down with your Being of Light on the marble steps.
- Feel its love and light all around you. Spend time connecting with this energy.
- This Being of Light has a message for you. Can you sense or hear what it is saying?
- Allow a few minutes to hear what this being is saying to you.
- Allow yourself to ask the Being of Light the answers to any pressing questions you may have.
- After you have received your answers, ask the Being of Light if it has any further insights for you.
- Allow yourself to thank the Being of Light and start to make your way back across the lawn to the door that you came in through.
- Ask the Being of Light if it is staying here in the vicinity of the Great Hall, or is it returning to Earth with you.
- Either way, bring the love of this Being of Light with you as you step into the galaxy and shut the door behind you.
- Feel yourself floating down through the galaxy and closer into the Earth's atmosphere. Move towards the building where your body lies.
- Connect once again with your body and ground completely into it.
- Gently move your hands and toes and reconnect with Earth's floor again.
- Take a deep breath and when you are ready, slowly open your eyes.

CHAPTER SEVENTEEN

Spiritual Awareness and Your Physical Life

ST GERMAIN:

Throughout the pages of this book the Beings of Light have opened many doorways of awareness. These doorways will never close and are only an introduction into other doorways. Over this life you will continue to explore these possibilities in your own time and as a result you will continue to connect to higher and higher levels of yourself. Throughout this exploration and learning, it is very important to also become aware of integrating your spiritual awareness into daily life. The following is a summary and in some cases an expansion of many of the principles and tools the Masters and Spiritual Family have discussed through the writings.

I, St Germain do speak to you through this section of the writings for it is part of my task upon Earth's floor to assist humans to anchor spiritual light into the Earth itself as well as into all that they create in their lives. I speak of the simplicity and the complexity of spirituality. Spirituality in essence is a very simple truth, it is the gentle beat of the universal drum. Spirituality can also be very complex in the sense that it can piece together a divinely intricate web of creation, life and mystery. I, St Germain find spiritual life to be in its strongest light when the simplicity and the complexity are in balance - equal portions of both.

A spiritual student will always be drawn to the teachings of the complex, intricate, detailing of the universe, but equally drawn to the gentle peace spirituality brings in its simplest form. Gratitude and acknowledgment, kindness and well wishing are among the simplest and strongest forms of the spiritual path. All religions of the world teach this gentle spirituality, these fundamental values, for all teachings come back to the one truth that is the core heart of the spiritual light that lives in all things. I attempt in my following writings to aid you by presenting ideas to integrate the rather complex teachings into the simplest day-to-day format so that you may balance your spirituality to achieve your divine goals of this incarnation.

Keys to Deepening Your Spiritual Life

What is Spiritual Life?

First, it is important to integrate your understanding of spiritual life by writing down, discussing or contemplating what spiritual life is to you. This is your path. It is essential that your spiritual life and path is completely yours. Rather than it being a thought, idea or example from another that holds very little meaning for you, carve out your own path according to what your heart calls you to do. It is through truly creating your spiritual path that it becomes yours and a part of you. As you own it in this way, it is an extension of you and you of it. It is yours. You will tend to it, dedicate to it and live it because it is a living energy in its own right, a manifestation of your spirit. Spend time on this question, "What is spiritual life?" and you will begin to understand its full meaning for you. All aspects of your life will become keys to your spiritual development, even the most mundane and ordinary tasks and issues.

What are the Benefits of Building a Spiritual Life?

When individuals work to create a stable foundation they build a home life and/or working life, social life and activities so as to keep passion and interest in living. If they have a family, they work to ensure the financial security of the family and endeavour to be helpful and useful in the extended family and community. For the most part, this is considered a happy life. Why then, do so many people seem unhappy with such a plan? Others, seeing the result of the plan, believe they can safeguard against unhappiness and try to make changes such as earning more money, not having children, travelling overseas, educating themselves or living alternatively in some way.

Regardless of the alterations to the formula, the individual comes to the point where they have established their framework for life but feel unfulfilled as though there must be something more. For some, the awareness of being unfulfilled does not come quite so easily and may follow a personal crisis or trauma. Whether it is a smooth transition into this level of awareness or a painful one, it is here that the individual may choose the spiritual path. They realise that finding happiness may not be solely based on making changes to external things. A faint urge or calling emerges from within and grows louder and stronger by the day. Those that listen to this calling and allow it to guide their next move find the doorway of spiritual awakening.

Although they may experience fear, they long to walk through that door. There is a level of nervous apprehension mixed with excitement. They can feel that the key to happiness and fulfilment is close. They crave every bit of information they can get their hands on as a way of speeding up the awakening procedure. Messages may start to come in dreams or through interesting people who cross their path. Where they used to walk around with eyes closed, now they insist on having them open. As a result, they begin to notice the many signs the universe sends them every day. These signs contribute to awakening, connecting, reminding and teaching the initiate. Their Higher Self gently makes its presence known and the initiate begins to realise that there is more to them than their external measure. The initiate is in fact a spiritual being in a human body, awakening to his/her true nature.

As time goes by, the initiate learns that spiritual life does not require the relinquishing of 'normal' everyday life in order to develop itself. Rather, the spiritual principles and sense of connectedness that create spiritual life ask to be integrated into the normal life already in operation. As one embraces spirituality one does not necessarily need to radically alter existing aspects of life, but to allow spirituality to enrich and nurture that which is already operating. A marriage for example, does not need to cease to be a union because one partner awakens spiritually. The partner can ask spirit to teach them how to use this new light to move the union forward in healing and in harmony.

If changes do occur in the foundational structure of the initiate's life when spirituality is embraced, these can often be the inevitable results of choosing a higher form of human expression. It is always important to remember that if changes do occur, once you are aligned to your higher will, the changes are always for your highest benefit. Through inviting spirituality into your life, your life becomes a Spiritual Life. You do not have to leave your life and adopt an entirely new life in order to create a spiritual life.

The benefits of spiritual life are endless, but most of all you move into a new level of appreciation and awareness of the divine beauty of each and every moment of your life - food tastes better, roses smell divine: you experience rather than exist.

For Spiritual Life, Develop a Tool Box

Spiritual life can be developed through embracing certain techniques that strengthen and enhance your sense of connectedness to your inner self and the Higher Realms. Your intuition will guide you when to use the tools below according to your own needs.

Writing

For many initiates, what starts off as journal writing can end up being channelled writing. Through writing, We that are of the Guides and Guardians for humanity can direct our messages into the initiate and have them come out through the pen and onto the paper. We can also channel through those initiates preferring to use the keyboard. Writing in your journal is a great way to open up your channels as it strengthens the certain areas of your mind that we use for channelling. Writing in all its forms is a powerful healer. Whether you are writing for creative purposes or to air a problem, write regularly as it releases stress and tension from the mind to make way for your guides to work with you.

Meditation

Use any form of meditation you find to be most beneficial and effective. We have suggested meditations in this book that you may wish to read onto a tape and play back to yourself. We do not have judgements on what is the best form of meditation as we can see that different meditations work for different people. The most important thing to note is that everyone can meditate, however some people believe they cannot. Meditation, like many other things, develops with practice. Dedicate yourself to this area of your journey and feed it with your time and energy when you can. You will find that in time the rewards will surprise you.

Prayer

Your prayers can be in whatever format you choose. There is no set style or form of prayer better than another. The most important aspect of prayer is the intention behind it. We receive permission from you to aid you not only by what you say in prayer, but the energy behind it. We feel the strength of your heart and your true desire to connect and we know what you are meaning regardless of what words you use. Words are still beneficial in anchoring your intention, however try not to worry about whether the words are 'right' or not. Some people use 'feeling prayers' where they spend time feeling our love for them or their love for us, and build the connection in this energetic way. This can be a very powerful form of manifestation when it is used in specific ways; for example, 'feeling happy prayers' where you simply spend time in prayer feeling happy.

Spending Time in Nature

The natural world will always be one of the strongest and most powerful healers for humankind. Humanity need only to reconnect to the natural world for many of the issues that feel like mountains to dissolve down to barely mounds. This connection is as simple as spending time in nature regularly. Most people do not understand the full power of nature. It has the ability to fast-track your healing process in an astonishing way. Each and every part of nature is a healer from the most ancient and tallest tree to the smallest flower. By appreciating nature you open your heart to it. As your heart opens to nature it opens to the healing force within nature. This force can remove the deepest pains and strongest fears.

Incorporate 'nature time' in your spiritual program. Whether you walk in nature, swim, write, meditate, contemplate or pray, the time spent has extraordinary value.

Invite nature into your home through encouraging sunlight into your rooms. Where possible plant trees and in meditation invite the birds to come to your sanctuary. Spend time with your hands in the dirt by making pot plants if you are a city dweller and plan weekend nature excursions where appropriate.

Growing your own vegetables and fruits is a wonderful way to feel connected to Mother Nature. It allows you to move in tune with the natural cycles. If you are limited in your ability to grow your own foods, eat organically where possible or keep a pot plant garden with herbs.

Reading Material, Tapes and CD's

The right books, tapes and CD's for you will call you. They will almost leap out at you from the shelves in the shop or they will be given to you by a friend or associate. Some people will be drawn to suggest books to you as they will intuitively know that the book has keys in it to trigger your memory of who you are and why you are on the planet. The spiritual path is very much about trusting your intuition so use it to guide you to the right material.

Support

Spiritual development is always aided by developing specific support networks. It is wise to observe those in your life who are supportive or unsupportive. For in the midst of spiritual challenge it makes all the difference if you are surrounded by people who will nurture you through periods of self-doubt or when you are tempted to abort the spiritual path. Those who are willing to encourage and counsel you will ensure that you reach your goals, even when it is you that wishes to scrap the plan! You will find that over time your energy will more willingly draw you to people who are supportive of you rather than those who choose a negative or pessimistic viewpoint. We are not suggesting that you cease to associate with negative or unsupportive people. We are suggesting that you will naturally select a network of people over time that will support you and you, them.

Your network may consist of a number of people. Among these may be a non-judgemental close confidante or friend, someone who is objective, compassionate and honest. In turn, you may be that person for another. You may find a close group to meditate or discuss things with and you may from time to time seek the help of a trusted counsellor or spiritual healer. Your support network may include a partner and other family members that are on a similar path. It is important to remember that a person does not have to hold the same beliefs as you in order to be part of your network, as often different views can be very enriching. You may also include a religious leader in your support group where necessary and appropriate.

Support can have other meanings aside from people in a network. 'Support' can mean to develop activities or practices that support your spiritual path. For some this is yoga, swimming, dancing or even a book club. It is something that helps you to feel good about yourself by anchoring a fresh new perspective in you.

CHAPTER EIGHTEEN

Conclusion

THE SPIRITUAL HIERARCHY FOR EARTH:

To conclude The Light-Worker's Companion, We that are of the Spiritual Hierarchy for Earth thank you. We thank you for sharing in this opportunity to educate and spread the word to others. As you read through the material in this book, it telepathically travels outwardly from your mind into the collective unconscious. This has worked to raise the vibration of humanity's consciousness.

This Universal Law works for every thought you have. Your positive thoughts travel into the collective unconscious and raise its vibration. As you continue to work through the exercises and lessons in this book or move onto study other books of higher consciousness, remember that every time you raise your vibration, you aid others. As you heal, so does humanity collectively heal. Thank you for contributing to raising the vibration of humanity.

We that are of the Spiritual Hierarchy for Earth will maintain our connection with you always, for in truth, we are all One.

And thus is this now done, in accordance to the Law of One, that does say this to We: When all are allowed to be within their frequencies, all shall come into peace and harmony.

And thus is this now complete, *Amen, amen, amen*

APPENDIX

Suggestions on the Use of Aromatherapy Oils for Spiritual Development

Basil
Has the ability to transmute deep levels of fear. Basil delves into layers of the emotional and mental body to aid the initiate to transmute fear that has built up over time. Basil transmutes anxiety that stems from fear.

Cardamom Seed
Assists in developing a bridge of connection between the initiate and the Higher Realms and Higher Self. Aids in spiritual connection.

Cinnamon
Can be mixed with water and sprayed in the energy field for spiritual protection. Shelters the energy field from negativity. Can be burnt in an oil burner in rooms that seem to attract lower vibrations.

Geranium
Assists to re-establish energetic boundaries in energy fields of people who have had these boundaries broken. This is useful in abuse cases where the individual has had certain rights taken from them. A child who has been abused may not be able to determine what her rights are because the energy

field has not been allowed to mature naturally. She may manifest abusive situations in her adult life partly because the energy field cannot read what is 'normal' or beneficial.

Geranium builds up the layers in the energy field that are weak and repairs breaks in the aura and energy fields. This is very good to use after surgery where the energy field has been disrupted. Put a few drops onto your hands and smooth it over the energy field as though you are building the layers with your hands.

Jasmine

A feminine energy, Jasmine brings comfort and security. Relieves nervous tension and brings a gentle but strong feminine influence into a situation. Jasmine is sometimes part of a scent used by Beings of Light and angels when they enter the room to relax individuals and let them know they are safe.

Lavender

The Lavender acts as an antiseptic for the energy field. Cleanses and nurtures. Lavender has so many spiritual properties and is considered so well rounded that if you are unsure what oils to use, Lavender is possibly your safest bet.

Lemongrass

A strong cleanser for the energy field. Lemongrass strips the energy field of layers of energetic debris or pollution. Can also be used to assist people to cleanse their energy fields after choosing to give up using Marijuana or any other addictive substance.

Lime

Assists access to the Higher Mind of the Higher Self. Promotes higher thought forms and uplifts the mental and emotional bodies.

Mandarin

Assists people through periods of grieving. Lifts the energy of grief from the emotional body and lightens the emotional load.

Orange

The Orange will lift the emotional body and cleanse it of heavy emotional residue. Can bring vitality and energy to the emotional, mental and physical body. Assists in lifting depression.

Rose

Helpful to burn or bathe in when transmuting anger. Rose transmutes anger and resentment and can relieve irritability and intolerance. It can also assist to build self-esteem. Placing Rose directly onto the heart chakra will encourage it to open up and develop deeper feelings of self-love.

Rosemary

Rosemary removes lower vibrations in the mental field that contribute to depressive thoughts.

Sandalwood

Can be used to encourage the opening and development of the crown chakra and channels contained within the crown. Can be placed on other chakra points to encourage them to respond to higher frequencies.

Definition of Terms

Aspects: Internal Characters or parts of oneself. If the Soul is a small pool of water, the aspects are each drop of water that makes up the pool. Each drop of water is as important as the other as each drop comes together to make the whole. Likewise, it is essential to the overall wellbeing of the 'pool' that each drop of water is as clear as possible. Any pollution in a single drop of water will pull down the vibration of the whole pool. Hence the importance of Aspect Therapy as a way of cleansing the individual drops of water or Aspects of Self.

Aspect therapy: Integration of all our internal characters. Integration of sub personalities. A Therapy to cleanse the individual aspects to ensure that they work in harmony with the whole.

Blueprints: When the spirit/aspect enters into the womb and into its physical form, prior to its birth, it brings with it a divine plan. This divine plan is a blueprint created by the Incarnation Council. Contained in the blueprint is the information the aspect requires throughout its life. This blueprint is like an internal navigation system that leads the human through the various stages and choices that present upon the life path.

Body cell memory: All physical experiences are stored in the memory banks of the body. These memory banks or store houses are located in the cells of the body. The cells store physical memories in their memory banks. The physical experiences of the body are stored to become a Body Cell Memory.

For example, if a Tom is in a car accident at 18 months old, he may not remember this accident. The body, however does remember and will store the memory in the store houses in the cells. Tom may have anxiety later in life but may not understand its origin. He can feel fear deep within his body and may need some assistance to locate the source of the fear.

Body cell memories – the cleansing of: Body cell memories can be cleared out through communicating with the cells and asking them to release their trauma. This can be done through the use of meditation and working with the Beings of Light. Regularly in meditation ask your cells to release trauma and see the Angelic Beings entering into your cells to remove all that no longer serves your highest good.

Body cell memory, blueprints and past lives: The blueprint has the ability to merge with the Body Cell Memory so that the memories contained in the blueprint are passed into the Body Cell Memory. This is relevant in cases where the Incarnation Council has encoded past life memory in the blueprint. The current human body of the incarnate is able to remember the past lives of the person.

This is why when clearing a past life memory of being hanged, for example, the body may physically manifest pains around the neck, feelings of throat restriction and overwhelming fear. The current body remembers what occurred in the past body because the memories have been transferred over into the new cells through the blueprint.

Chakras: Powerful energy centres primarily in the human body. These centres are spinning vortexes of energy that can be developed to assist in the Ascension process. The major chakras are found at the top of the head, forehead, throat, central chest, solar plexus, lower abdomen and coccyx. Each chakra is associated with a different colour and is connected to particular spiritual attributes.

Channels: Channels live within a person's crown chakra, feet and hands. All chakras of the body contain channels. These channels allow for information and energy to flow throughout the human system. Channel systems are also found in the etheric realms above and below a person. These etheric channels create the link to higher dimensions, and to the

Earth and sea. There are channel systems in the heart chakra to connect humanity together and to bridge humanity with nature and animals.

Channel systems: A channel system can be likened to a complex matrix of millions of optic fibres. Information travels through these 'optic fibres' from one port to another. The feminine aspect of your mind (the Lunar Mind) receives the information sent through these 'optic fibres' to you. Your Lunar Mind is best described as a port that is linked to many other ports throughout the galaxy. For example, you may be connected to the port of St Germain. This means that you will receive transmissions from his port that are relevant to you and compatible with your frequency bands. These thousands of optic fibres (the channel system) you are working through hook themselves into your port (Lunar Mind). Your channels receive the messages and if you are connected to your Lunar Mind, you receive the messages also.

You may have for example, a channel system that is linked to the Council of Ascended Masters. This means that you will be able to receive messages from that council when required. It is possible to have many different channel systems connected to different beings, realms and dimensions running simultaneously. Such connections may include the Sea Realms, the Angelic Realm – to the Archangels or to specific guides. The question arises, 'How does the channel differentiate the information?' The answer to this question is that the channel system itself has a 'sorting out section' where it files and organises messages. This is why to people who channel can often feel as though there is a line up of guides waiting to talk. Information is lined up rather than all thrown in together.

A channel system also has the ability to translate information that may have come from different parts of the galaxy or telepathically from people across the other side of the world that do not speak your language. For example, a person can channel His Holiness the Dalai Lama in meditation when the person speaks only English. The channel system will automatically convert data to your understanding and language.

Channelling: Channelling is receiving messages or higher information. It is the process of receiving information through the Lunar Mind (feminine aspect of the mind). Information is generally transmitted from the Lunar Mind to you through telepathic exchange or intuitive awareness.

Channelling can also be received through automatic writing, visions, sounds, drawings, and through sensations and feelings that bring a knowing. A common form of channelling is instant perception where a person instantly understands something as though the clue has been dropped into their mind.

Channelling – 'Walk Throughs': A less common form of channelling that requires a mention is 'Walk Throughs'. A Walk Through is where a person allows another Being of Light to move into their physical body to deliver a message or perform a healing. The being temporarily moves into the physical body of the person channelling. The person may not remember what has been said and may experience going into a different space or state while the message or healing is being transmitted.

Christ Consciousness: Christ Consciousness is a force and source of Light. It is a consciousness in its own right, but is connected to and part of the eternal Oneness. It is often perceived as Golden Light as it has an illuminating and brightening effect and is connected to and a part of the Great Central Sun.

Christ Consciousness and the Great Central Sun: The Great Central Sun is a centre of light, healing and ascension for many planets and realms throughout the galaxy. There is a Higher Council within the Great Central Sun that assists humanity and Mother Earth regularly. The council is one of many that are facilitating the shift of Mother Earth and all those on Earth so choosing, to ascend into the dimensions of Love and Light. The Great Central Sun Higher Council specialises in such things as planetary and individual ascension as well as the transmutation of fear.

Calling on the Christ Consciousness to enter every cell of your body in meditation and before you fall asleep is a very powerful exercise. By doing this you allow the Christ Consciousness to work in your body to transmute fear and lower vibrational frequencies. This higher energy will prepare you for ascension and make your job a lot easier. The Christ Consciousness is able to live within each level of you including your Hierarchy. It bases itself within the Sun Level of your Hierarchy, but is designed to extend down into all levels.

Christ Consciousness Higher Council: There are many Beings of Light that sit on the Christ Consciousness Higher Council. Lord Sananda, an aspect of Lord Jesus the Christ sits on the council alongside Lord Buddha, St Germain, Lord Mohammad, Lady Mary Magdalene, Mother Mary and many others. The Christ Consciousness Higher Council meetings are open to all beings who have attained Christ Consciousness.

Councils: Higher Councils, Councils of Light. Councils are groups of Light Beings gathered in equality with the intention to assist in governing specific areas of Earth, humanity, and the galaxy for the highest good and will of all.

Dimensions: Realms of vibrational existence.

Etheric body, etheric vision, etheric plane: The etheric body is the energetic body/field around a human body. The etheric body is found outside the auric field. The auric field is closer to Earth and is denser than the etheric field. Aspects of fear and the personality of an individual can be found in the auric field. The etheric body is a light body and a bridge that the Higher Self uses to connect to the human self. Contained within the etheric body are higher frequencies, colours, sounds, telepathic abilities and the gift of etheric vision. Etheric vision allows the initiate to see on a higher plane whilst travelling in their etheric body. This, and the telepathic ability, is why the etheric body is used in meditation. The etheric plane is the reality where an initiate can communicate with and see the Ascended Masters. An initiate travels to an etheric plane in the etheric body to receive higher teachings and training from the Beings of Light. When you do some of the meditations in this book, you are using and strengthening your own etheric tools and abilities.

Etheric realms: Etheric realms are realities that do not have the density and solidity that Earth has. These realms may seem almost transparent and light whereas Earth appears very solid. Because of the lack of density in these realms, beings living in etheric realms do not have the physical restrictions that humans have on Earth. Etheric beings do not require food consumption to the degree of human bodies and do not experience sickness and ageing as a process of deterioration. Some etheric realms co-exist with Earth and can been seen and visited by humans when they enter the meditative or dream state. Humans can experience etheric realms by leaving behind their physical bodies and travelling in their etheric bodies. Some initiates train to master this ability through their lives and do this by transmuting the density in their physical form. This is achieved through dedication to meditation, releasing of fear and negativity, and caring for their human body.

Frequency: A set vibration of colour, sound and light.

Human Initiate or an 'Initiate': A spiritual being that has incarnated in human form for the purpose of or intention to Ascend or spiritually awaken. A person in some form of spiritual training.

Keys: Information banks of higher technology, colour, sound, light and memory. These information banks are encoded into a person's body or places in the Earth. These are released in a person's body or areas on Earth when the area or individual is moving into a new vibration or higher frequency. Contained within the key is often a memory of themselves in a past time or how to do something they couldn't previously do. For example, you may travel to a sacred site on Earth and whilst there, have a key released in you. You may find for the months afterward, memories activate of times that you have spent there in previous incarnations. Abilities you had in that life may return to you and aid you in your personal/spiritual development in this life. You may find that you have new channels available to you and your meditations have shifted into a higher frequency.

Light-Worker: A person on Earth who has made a prior agreement before incarnating or enters into a level of training to:
- Awaken to higher levels of awareness and connect to higher frequencies.
- Be of service to the higher development of humanity and/or Earth, nature.
- Use the keys, gifts, tools and abilities they incarnated with to aid themselves and others for the highest good of all.

A Light-Worker is a Being of Light that incarnates specifically to reach a higher level of spiritual awareness and aid others to do the same in the process. This may not always look the way one would expect. Light-Workers work in all different professions and some not necessarily in professions at all. The Spiritual Hierarchy for Earth places Light-Workers in all places and walks of life. Light-Workers are the shining lights amongst the darkness, the guiding lights in a family, and the caring ones in the corporate world. They exist on Earth to guide humanity into another way, to show the way into a more loving way of living and being.

Lunar Mind: The feminine aspect of your mind responsible for allowing channelled information to reach you. The Lunar Mind receives all higher inspiration and divine guidance.

Every person on Earth's floor has a Lunar Mind and is connected to their Hierarchy. Because of these factors, everyone has the ability to channel. A person can choose not to channel by refusing to consciously connect to their Lunar Mind. A person can also choose not to have conscious awareness of their Hierarchy or Higher Self.

Because the Lunar Mind is the feminine aspects of the mind, connection can be made by removing yourself from intense logical and analytical exploration into allowing and trust. Allowing and trust is developed through becoming in tune with yourself and your essential nature. Meditation, prayer, writing, and spending time in nature are powerful tools to use when developing a connection with your Lunar Mind. The feminine aspects of your mind are in essence, creative and intuitive. By allowing your creative self to express, you are exercising parts of your Lunar Mind.

Memory banks: Memory banks are storehouses for memories; feelings, thoughts, experiences and information. These memory banks are found at the cellular level of a person. Data from previous incarnations can be stored in a memory bank. This data can be triggered by the people, places or experiences of this life, thus activating past life recollection in an individual.

Soul: A Soul is the Oneness beyond the Hierarchy as well as the whole Hierarchy and all aspects contained within it. If the Soul is a vibrant sun, the Hierarchy is the massive shaft of light extending down from the sun, and the aspects are the small particles of light contained in the shaft of light. In truth the sun, its shaft of light and its light particles are all one.

Spiritual Hierarchy for Earth: The Spiritual Hierarchy for Earth was formed before Earth's creation. It is the governing body of the planet.

In my understanding, the Spiritual Hierarchy for Earth consists of twelve founding individual Hierarchies. As Earth developed, interest in her grew and thus the Spiritual Hierarchy for Earth received new individual members from different parts of the galaxy, however the founding members remain and are the core of the governing body.

POSTSCRIPT

St Germain

I, St Germain and all of us that have contributed to this work from the 'higher planes' do now come forth and send our love and blessings to you. We remind you that we will stand beside you through all phases of your spiritual journey. We thank you for the honour and opportunity to be of service to you through this work and do say to you to call on us regularly and through this permission we shall aid you directly.

All our love to you, *Amen, amen, amen.*

OTHER BOOKS BY AMANDA GUGGENHEIMER

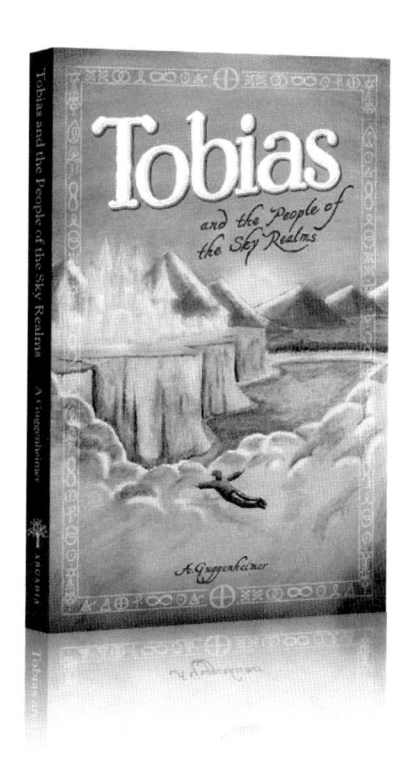

Tobias and the People of the Sky Realms

When an ethereal stranger climbed through Tobias's bedroom window in the middle of the night, the young man had no idea that she came to claim him for a vital mission. Her world, in the Sky Realms above earth, suffered from a dark enemy. That enemy lived on earth and also worked to enslave human minds.

After visiting the Sky Realms, Tobias realises he has little choice but to help his new friend and her family. The future of the Sky Realms and earth depended upon it. In battle, he prays for the courage to do what is expected of him, not realising that a long-lost part of himself, caught in another time, could undermine the entire mission.

For more information please visit www.arcadiapress.com.au

- The Secret of Shambhala by James Redfield (prayer feilds)
- Tibetan Monk Chanting disc
- Jennifer Farmer